THE BUSINESS OF TRAINING

Further titles in the McGraw-Hill Training Series

EVALUATING TRAINING EFFECTIVENESS
Translating Theory into Practice
Peter Bramley ISBN 0-07-707331-2

DEVELOPING EFFECTIVE TRAINING SKILLS
Tony Pont ISBN 0-07-707383-5

MAKING MANAGEMENT DEVELOPMENT WORK
Achieving Success in the Nineties
Charles Margerison ISBN 0-07-707382-7

MANAGING PERSONAL LEARNING AND CHANGE
A Trainer's Guide
Neil Clark ISBN 0-07-707344-4

HOW TO DESIGN EFFECTIVE TEXT-BASED OPEN LEARNING: A Modular Course
Nigel Harrison ISBN 0-07-707355-X

HOW TO DESIGN EFFECTIVE COMPUTER BASED TRAINING: A Modular Course
Nigel Harrison ISBN 0-07-707354-1

HOW TO SUCCEED IN EMPLOYEE DEVELOPMENT
Moving from Vision to Results
Ed Moorby ISBN 0-07-707459-9

Details of these and other titles in the series are available from:

The Product Manager, Professional Books, McGraw-Hill Book Company (UK) Limited, Shoppenhangers Road, Maidenhead, Berkshire, SL6 2QL.
Telephone: 0628 23432 Fax: 0628 770224

The business of training

Achieving success in changing world markets

Trevor Bentley

McGRAW-HILL BOOK COMPANY

London · New York · St Louis · San Francisco · Auckland
Bogotá · Caracas · Hamburg · Lisbon · Madrid · Mexico · Milan
Montreal · New Delhi · Panama · Paris · San Juan · São Paulo
Singapore · Sydney · Tokyo · Toronto

Published by
McGRAW-HILL Book Company (UK) Limited
Shoppenhangers Road, Maidenhead, Berkshire SL6 2QL, England.
Telephone 0628 23432
Fax 0628 770224

British Library Cataloguing in Publication Data
Bentley, Trevor J.
The business of training
1. Personnel. Training
I. Title
658.3124

ISBN 0-07-707328-2

Library of Congress Cataloging-in-Publication Data
Bentley, Trevor J.
The business of training/Trevor J. Bentley.
p. cm.—(The McGraw-Hill training series)
Includes bibliographical references and index.
ISBN 0-07-707328-2
1. Employees—Training of. I. Title. II. Series.
HF5549.5.T7B455 1990
658.3'124—dc20 90-6464

2345 BP 94321

Typeset by Book Ens Limited, Baldock, Herts
Printed and bound in Great Britain by The Bath Press, Avon

To my son CLIVE without whose guidance I would never have re-discovered my inherent learning skills

Contents

Page

Series preface xi
About the series editor xiii
Introduction **xv**
A vision of the future that leads towards the realization that investing in people through training is the direct path to corporate success.

PART ONE: **The changing world of training**

1 **The changing workplace** **3**
This chapter explores the impact that rapid changes have on training, covering changing patterns of work, the speed of change and the skills gap, and the problems for individuals, organizations and economies.

2 **Change management** **8**
Success, both individual and corporate, depends upon the ability of people to adapt to change. There are several agents of change that can lead to human obsolescence. The importance of giving people support at work is critical to successful change management.

3 **The psychology of training for success** **13**
Things get in the way of personal success, particularly psychological barriers. Positive motivation and ways to overcome psychological barriers are important aspects of good training.

PART TWO: **The business of training**

4 **The strategic role of training** **21**
The link between people and profits is clear. Developing a skilled workforce through becoming a learning organization with a learning culture is vital for success. Performance and profits are closely linked and need effective training strategies for corporate success.

5 **Developing a training strategy for the future** **27**
To make the best use of the training, investment training must be a major part of the corporate strategy. Implementing the training strategy can be done in a variety of ways, centralized, de-centralized, or distributed; these all have advantages and disadvantages.

15 Learning environments **117**
The three environments in which people learn are discussed. The living environment, the working environment, and the education and training environment. For training to be successful good learning environments have to be created.

PART SIX: **High technology in training**

16 New training tools **125**
In this chapter four training tools are described, Embedded Computer Based Training (ECBT), Concurrent Computer Based Training (CCBT), expert systems, and intelligent tutors.

17 Computer screen standards **136**
It is suggested that continuous training and support is more effective if there is a good interface between people and machines. This chapter sets out some standards that will improve the user interface.

18 Electronic performance support systems **142**
Gloria Gery, an American consultant, describes a new concept in supporting people at work. The qualities of EPSS, and the basic conditions for the development of EPSS are covered, together with its benefits.

19 Performance management systems **150**
Three levels of performance, corporate, personal, and training, are looked at, as is the process of creating a performance management system. Attribute analysis and the development of cost benefit models are examined, together with the idea of maximizing people power.

Glossary of terms 157

Note 163

Suggested reading 165

Index 167

Series preface

Training and development are now firmly centre stage in most organizations, if not all. Nothing unusual in that—for some organizations. They have always seen training and development as part of the heart of their business. More and more must see it the same way.

The pressure is on for them to do so. This pressure is coming from varied sources. The government, the CBI, the unions, the BIM, the new TECs, the EC and foreign competition are all exerting pressure—not just for more training, but for more relevant, appropriate and useful training.

In addition, the demographic trends through the nineties will inject into the market place severe competition for good people who will need good training. Young people without conventional qualifications, skilled workers in redundant crafts, people out of work, women wishing to return to work—all will require excellent training to fit them to meet the job demands of the 1990s and beyond.

But excellent training does not spring from what we've done well in the past. T&D specialists are in a new ball-game. 'Maintenance' training—to keep up skill-levels to do what we've always done—will be less in demand. Rather, organization, work and market change training are now much more important and will remain so for some time. Changing organizations and people is no easy task, requiring special skills and expertise which, sadly, many T&D specialists do not possess.

To work as a 'change' specialist requires us to get to centre stage—to the heart of the company's business. This means we have to ask about future goals and strategies and even be involved in their development, at least as far as T&D policies are concerned.

This demands excellent communication skills, political expertise, negotiating ability, diagnostic skills—indeed, all the skills a good internal consultant requires.

The implications for T&D specialists are considerable. It is not enough merely to be skilled in the basics of training, we must also begin to act like business people and to think in business terms and talk the language of business. We must be able to resource training not just from within but by using the vast array of external resources. We must be able to manage our activities as well as any other manager. We must share in the creation and communication of the company's vision. We must never let the goals of the company out of our sight.

In short, we may have to grow and change with the business. It will be hard. We shall have to demonstrate not only relevance but also value for money and achievement of results. We shall be our own boss, as accountable for results as any other line manager, and we shall have to deal with fewer internal resources.

The challenge is on, as many T&D specialists have demonstrated to me over the past few years. We need to be capable of meeting that challenge. This is why McGraw-Hill Book Company (UK) Limited have planned and launched this major new training series—to help us meet that challenge.

The series covers all aspects of T&D and provides the knowledge base from which we can develop plans to meet the challenge. They are practical books for the professional person. They are a starting point for mapping out our journey into the twenty-first century.

Use them well. Don't just read them. Highlight key ideas, thoughts, action pointers or whatever, and have a go at doing something with them. Through experimentation we evolve, through stagnation we die.

I know that all the authors in the McGraw-Hill Training Series would want me to wish you good luck. Have a great journey into the twenty-first century.

ROGER BENNETT
Series Editor

About the series editor

Roger Bennett has over twenty years' experience in training, management education, research and consulting. He has long been involved with trainer training and trainer effectiveness. He has carried out research into trainer effectiveness and conducted workshops, seminars and conferences on the subject around the world. He has written extensively on the subject including the book *Improving Trainer Effectiveness*, Gower. His work has taken him all over the world and has involved directors of companies as well as managers and trainers.

Dr Bennett has worked in engineering, several business schools (including the International Management Centre, where he launched the UK's first master's degree in T&D) and has been a board director of two companies. He is the editor of the *Journal of European Industrial Training* and was series editor of the ITD's *Get In There* workbook and video package for the managers of training departments. He now runs his own business called The Management Development Consultancy.

Introduction

The vision I have sees training at the centre of the stage—no longer the Cinderella in the corporate household. It sees investment in people being recognized as the most important investment that can be made, and it sees the wide application of advanced computer technology in delivering and managing this investment.

My vision also sees people taking control of their own growth and development, demanding training time and money as part of their just rewards for supplying their services. It also sees management recognizing the need to apply the basic principles of learning in their everyday work, and a greater emphasis on performance-related training investment. It sees the whole organization becoming a vehicle for the learning and growth of people.

The rapidly changing workplace of the future will demand that trainers move towards this vision with a spirit of adventure. Training professionals at all levels will have to display considerable imagination, common sense and creativity to cope with the changes that undoubtedly await us.

Why should the future bring such a revolution in corporate attitudes to change? The answer is, I believe, quite simple. Corporate success depends upon having and keeping talented people. This is as true today as it has always been.

The shortage of such people is widely accepted, and training, at long last, is beginning to be recognized as part of the solution. The total investment in training is still pitifully small, but it is growing.

Another factor which will lead towards my vision, is the growing awareness among trainers of the close relationship between training and profit. More and more training professionals are realizing that it is necessary, and possible, to produce training investment appraisals which show the financial return from investing in training.

The expanding use of such techniques will clearly indicate to management the tremendous benefits that are achievable. This in turn will lead to training being more readily accepted as an investment rather than an expense.

Training is not, however, a 'one-off investment'. It is a continuing investment. Not only is it needed to create the skilled workforce, but also to maintain the high level of skills demanded by the ever-changing workplace.

The workplace has always been a changing enviroment, but never before have the changes been so extensive. The things people do, the way they do them, and their importance to the business are all changing rapidly. One of the primary causes of this exciting period of change has undoubtedly been the vast expansion in the development and application of computer technology. Automation in the factory and in the office has completely changed the complexion of work. Many traditional trades have disappeared, and new ones have arisen.

The realignment of the workforce has significantly changed the approach to education. The work ethic of a trade and a job for life is going. It is likely that individuals may have several different types of job during their working lives. Working lives will be shorter because of longer initial training and earlier retirement. During these shorter working lives people will have to undergo extensive periods of re-training.

This means that the task of creating and retaining a talented workforce, that can adjust to the changing work enviroment, should be a very high priority in the corporate strategy.

The computer has been around since 1946, but it is only in the last ten years that it has come out of the back room, where it was attended by specialists, and landed in everyone's workplace. If this is linked with the developments in communications that have occurred during the same time-frame, it becomes clear that there has been an explosion of technology.

This 'invasion' of high tech is going to continue, as the power, storage capacity and ease of use improve, and cost declines. Millions of people need to be trained in the effective use of the technology, and will then need to be updated continuously on the changes that will inevitably take place.

What is needed is some means whereby individuals can receive continuous updating and training, when they need it, when they ask for it, and delivered to them in their workplace, via the technology they use in their daily work. Meeting the aim of continuous training and support is becoming possible, by harnessing the very technology which is causing the changes to take place.

This book is about investing in people, and doing it so that the returns from the investment are substantial. This can be done by designing training that is centred on the learning process, and by using the best possible tools and techniques.

Of course to achieve my vision of training in the future, training professionals will need to develop much more comprehensive training management systems, and here again technology can come to the rescue.

The business of training is about making sure that the people on whom the organization depends are equipped with the knowledge and skills they need for handling a rapidly changing enviroment. It is about marrying the investment in training with the skill and imagination of people. It is about using the very best training approaches possible.

I would like to thank my friends and colleagues at Westpac Training Services Pty Ltd, Sydney, for their tolerance, willingness to experiment with ideas and to explore new ways of doing things. I would also like to thank my good friend Gloria Gery for her support, and for agreeing to my using her material on Electronic Performance Support Systems (Chapter 18), and to Weingarten Publications for permission to use Gloria's material which first appeared in CBT Directions.

There are many more people I have worked with in workshops in several different countries whom I would like to thank. These are people from who I have learned a great deal, much of which is reflected in this book. They know who they are so to all of you a big thank you.

TREVOR BENTLEY

PART ONE

The changing world of training

1 The changing workplace

Forty years ago a person could plan to follow a single career from leaving school until retirement. This is no longer the case. During their working lifetime people may well have to follow several career paths as their previous skills become obsolete. This rapid acceleration of the rate of change started with the introduction of computers in the late forties and early fifties. Though the changes were slow at first, and only affected a few people, they have now accelerated, and concern almost everyone.

This rapid rate of change means that it is no longer possible to 'learn a trade' that can be relied upon for a full working life. This reliance may be suitable for a few years, but then it will be necessary to start again and learn a new set of skills. This places a tremendous demand on the training resources of individual organizations, and means that everyone has to be ready to learn new things, and adapt to a different form of work, not once but continually.

Some of the most noticeable changes have been brought about by computers, and are concerned with three main aspects of work. Firstly there are changes in *the way people do things.* Secondly there are changes in *the things people do.* Thirdly there are the changes in *the way people think about work.*

The way people do things

People now work in quite different ways than in the past. This is noticeable in the office, the factory, the warehouse, and the retail shop. In fact it is noticeable everywhere. The introduction of word processors and personal computers has changed the way information is processed, and even who does the work, with many managers now typing their own correspondence and reports. Automated machines have replaced many of the skills in the factory, and now instead of setting and controlling machines by hand, the computer has taken over.

The things people do

The things people do have changed considerably: not only are old things being done in new ways, but completely new things are being done. The production of printed circuit boards and micro chips is an obvious example, as is the new 'software' industry, both for commercial and leisure activities. Even within more traditional industries such as steel making and car manufacture, the activities of the workforce have changed considerably. Instead of working in a hot and sometimes dangerous workplace, people now sit in white coats in the clean air-conditioned safety of the computer control room.

The way people think about work

Because people see no long-term future for any one particular skill they are less able to make a commitment to investing time, money, and effort in acquiring such skill. Apprenticeships are far less attractive than they used to be. By the time apprentices have completed their indenture their hard-earned skill is probably obsolete. Even in areas such as medicine, computing, and accounting people have to be willing to adapt quickly to the changing workplace.

More work is being done in the home, modern computers and communication systems making this quite realistic. There is more part-time work, and people are actually doing more than one job, or even job sharing. This potentially makes work much more interesting and varied, and gives scope for many more people to be self-employed.

All of this makes people think differently about work, about what they want to do, and about how they want to do it. There are ever-increasing opportunities for individuals to learn about, and work in the new industries that are slowly replacing the old. The implications for training are enormous.

The speed of change

Now none of this would present too much of a problem if the changes were occurring slowly, but they are not. The speed of change is getting faster, and it is unlikely that particular work skills will remain valid for much more than ten years, except for some activities such as 'silver service' in a restaurant or furniture removal. And there are some areas of work where the skills will change in less than five years.

This means that plans have to be made for everyone's continual training and updating. Refresher and updating courses will have to be a regular—at least annual—feature of everyone's future (see Chapter 14). For the organization that is going to invest in its people via training a radical new approach to training has to be instigated. The business of training means much more than just improving the present ways of training, it means looking at how people are going to be able to grow and develop to keep pace with what is happening in the real world, and at ways of creating a learning organization.

The skills gap

The majority of people aged fifty and over finished their education approximately thirty years ago, which was long before there was even the hint of the coming computer revolution. For the majority of people aged forty plus the story is similar. Twenty years ago they were aware of the growing role of computers, but had no idea of what was to come, and few if any educational establishments were including computer training in the curriculum. This means in effect that the vast majority of senior managers were never exposed to computers during the formative years of their development, and very few have taken any action to remedy this. Those people who finished their education even ten years ago, probably first met computers at university, rather than in the school classroom. It is only now that people are coming onto the job market who first met the computer in the primary school classroom, i.e. at the age of six or seven.

The net effect of this slowness of the educational system to adapt to the changing needs of society is that there is an enormous skills gap. This is reflected by the many vacancies waiting to be filled, and the large numbers of people who are unemployed because they have the wrong skills, and have received an inappropriate education. These skill gaps exist in most if not all of the developed countries.

Bridging the skills gap

The best place to start is with the education system, but this is so slow, and so bogged down by political dogma that people might as well put their efforts into adult training. This can be done in two ways: by providing learning opportunities linked to work, and by providing learning opportunities directly to the individual via both the private and the public sectors. This book is not concerned with the political implications of bridging the skills gap. What it is concerned with is the way in which organizations should plan for and provide training that ensures they will not suffer from shortages of skilled staff due to the skills gap.

No organization can or should wait for someone else to bridge the skills gap. If they do wait the result will be an organization always working on half power, without the people skills that are needed for success. Bridging the skills gap may not be as difficult as might be imagined as long as the organization takes care to see that its needs are carefully analysed and met by a comprehensive programme of continuous training (see Chapter 14).

Failure to keep pace

If skills fail to keep pace with the changing workplace, then the implications for individuals, for organizations, and for the economy will be significant.

Individuals

It is important that those responsible for human resource development should fully recognize that it is the knowledge, skills, attitudes, and behaviour of individuals that lead directly to corporate success. Individuals need to be encouraged to seek the kind of opportunities that they want, and encouraged to take every opportunity to develop and grow in the way they want, consistent with improving their own performance and contribution.

However, now and in the future, few individuals will be prepared to wait around for someone else to decide what is best for them. They will decide for themselves the training they want, and then they will make sure that they get it. Either they will persuade the organization they work for to provide it, or they will take steps or provide it for themselves. They may have to invest time, effort, and money in themselves—and where better?

There is no doubt in my mind, that both the private and the public sectors should be providing ample opportunity for adults to choose the type of personal growth and development that is right for them. Nor do I doubt that given suitable financial support the demand would be overwhelming.

It is interesting that the UK government have recently introduced a new loan scheme called the Career Development Loan. This scheme works by the individual arranging a loan for training with one of a specified group of banks. The interest on the loan is paid by the government for the duration of the course, and up to three months afterwards, at which point the individual has to pay back the loan and any further interest. The training must be job related. Loans from £300 to £5000 can be applied for, to cover up to 80 per cent of the cost of the course, which can last from one week to a year.

Organizations

For each organization the outcome is similar. Without the skills it needs it will be unable to keep up to date, and to compete effectively. The products and services produced will become unattractive and sales will fall. The productivity of the workforce will stagnate and fall behind that of competitors, thus increasing comparative costs. The effect will be for profits to fall, for less money to be available to invest in people and capital, and the organization will find itself on the slippery road to eventual demise. There really is no alternative than to make sure that the human skills so vital to success are developed and maintained (See Chapter 2).

The economy

For the economy of a country the net result will be an increase in the deficit on the balance of trade. If a country cannot develop a workforce with the required skills then it will need to buy those skills from abroad, or buy the products and services produced by those skills, and thus increase imports. At the same time because they lack the necessary skills home-produced products and services will not meet overseas customers' needs, and exports will fall. Unemployment will grow, and inflation will rise as interest rates increase to protect the currency. The effect will be to reduce the standard of living as a whole. A nation, any nation, succeeds on the basis of the skills of its people, both to innovate and produce the products and services it needs. Without those skills the result is entirely predictable, unless the country receives a windfall, as the UK did from North Sea oil.

Training is perhaps the most effective way to get out of the downward spiral, for individuals, organizations, and the economy. It will need an investment from everyone, but as can be seen in Chapter 16 the investment will pay off handsomely. There is no doubt in my mind that there are going to be even more far-reaching changes as technology develops. Investing in training for success is not only good sense, it is absolutely vital.

Key points

- Change is so fast that people need to train and re-train continuously.
- The way things are done is changing.
- The things people do are changing.

- The way people think about work is changing.
- There is an enormous skills gap.
- Individuals will seek the training they need.
- Organizations need to bridge the skills gap.
- Economies need to invest in developing human skills.
- Training is the way forward for individuals, organizations, and economies.

2 Change management

Successful people and successful organizations all display an ability to respond well to change. In fact most of the time they are the instigators of change. What is it that makes it possible for some people to react well to change? The first most obvious factors are that they are confident, self-assured and open minded. These are also features of people who learn well. Secondly change is seen by successful people as an opportunity, a challenge rather than a threat. Managing change becomes a major problem if the workforce and the organization are not equipped to handle change well. Change in itself is not a problem, it is the implication that the change has for people. The learning organization that encourages its workforce to learn and to grow as people will have little difficulty in managing change, even if the change has a significant impact on the things people do, and the way people do things.

Building the right attitudes to change and creating a responsive workforce are virtually the same process as building the learning organization. The more people are encouraged to experiment and explore their enviroment, the more they become open to new ideas and new ways to do things, in other words the more they become adaptable to change.

The process of learning is one of discovery and acceptance of new experiences. It is a process of constant change and growth. If this is encouraged, and if people are allowed to flourish in a protected and supportive environment, then attitudes to change will be good. Of course the opposite of this is also true, and organizations that react badly to change will almost certainly not be learning organizations. They will display rigid attitudes to work, and will not see training as a strategic activity for future growth.

Agents of change

In this section three main agents of change will be considered: these are social change, organizational change, and technological change.

Social change

Social change occurs gradually, and its effects are cumulative. Two of the most significant social changes that are taking place at the moment are the development of the independent woman with equal rights, and the switch from industrial work to information work. These affect everything about the way people live and the way they perceive the world around them. They affect the media, the products on the market, entertainment, education, and personal relationships. They affect people's wealth and status and through these the demands made on the market place. Banks now lend money to married women without demanding the husband's signature. Mortgages are now provided on the basis of joint salaries, and so on.

Naturally these implications reach into the workplace. There are training courses available now for assertiveness training for women, and they are very popular. As workers continue to move out of the factory and into the office there are more opportunities for women, and in the developed countries women form a much larger proportion of the workforce than twenty years ago.

Organizational change

The world today is one of constant organizational change. Takeovers and mergers are only one factor, re-grouping, re-organizations, and disinvestment are others that cause major upheaval in the workplace. Such changes bring with them uncertainties that many people feel unable to face. There are many people who seek a steady, secure enviroment in which to live and work, and organizational changes threaten these very things. Yet often, after the event, people say that it is the best thing that has happened to them.

In the learning organization people are much more ready to examine such changes from the viewpoint of what they will gain, rather than what they will lose. This makes organizational change easier to manage, and will bring greater benefits than similar changes in non-learning organizations. The ability to learn and grow is fundamental to handling change. If people are not allowed to use their inherent learning skills they feel frustrated, held back, and are rarely open to change.

Technological change

Technological change has been rapid and far reaching. People have found the move from desk-based paperwork to computers a traumatic experience. One of the reasons for this is because most people using the systems are trained to the minimum level necessary to use the system. The error rates in most systems are high and many people never seem completely comfortable with the computer system they are using.

Why is it that people have so much difficulty with a machine that should be very easy to use? I believe that one of the major problems stems from the system designers' concentration on what the system does, i.e. its functionality, rather than on the usability of the system. Of course functionality is important, but if the functions provided by the system can't be used then it is pretty pointless having them there in the first place. There is an urgent need for system designers to pay regard to the needs of the user for simple, easy-to-use systems. This is an important aspect of change management as more and more people move into 'information work'.

Computers and people

People use computers in a wide variety of ways, sometimes being unaware that they are using one. Cash dispensers are an example of this kind of use. But all too often users are confronted by the need to interact with the computer via a keyboard and screen. This interaction is managed by the software.

Information work relies on the effective use of computers, and this is ensured if systems are easy to use. An 'easy-to-use' system can be defined as one in which someone who has never used the system before is able to interact successfully with the system in easy-to-follow, and simple-to-understand steps. There should be no need for pre-training, and users should be able to ask the system for, and receive information about what they are doing at any time. To create such systems it is necessary for system designers to understand the psychology of human/machine interfacing. The interface between people and machines is not a thing, it is a point in time and space where the finger touches the key, and the eye reads the screen, and yet it is the key to building easy-to-use systems. But more of this later.

The impact of building 'easy-to-use' systems is considerable, because 'easy-to-use' systems are also 'easy-to-learn', efficient in operation, potentially error free, and far easier to implement. No matter how brilliantly systems are designed and built, if they are not 'easy to use' they will rarely, if ever, produce the anticipated returns. They will frustrate the successful introduction of change, even when people are highly adaptive.

Human obsolescence

One of the biggest problems of change management is the way that people with a particular set of skills can so easily become obsolete: not obsolete as people, but as particular kinds of workers. People who have worked hard to learn a trade can be shattered by the realization that nobody needs the knowledge and skills that they have to offer. Recent moves in the newspaper industry in the UK to eliminate composing and typesetting work by getting journalists to key their stories directly into the computer, have deeply divided workers, many of whom are now obsolete. This is not the only example. There are many instances in manufacturing where semi-skilled and skilled jobs have been replaced by technology, making the workers who possessed the skills obsolete.

The impact of human obsolescence is considerable, particularly for the workers themselves. The first effect is the feeling of being useless, of having no value to society. This is followed by the sense of being unable to provide for the needs of the family, which hits at the basic pride and esteem of all working people. Then come all the materialistic problems of simply not having the money to continue to live as before. All this pressure leads to illness, both mental and physical, and to a wide range of personal difficulties.

For society the situation becomes very difficult to handle. At one extreme are the obsolete workers who represent the new poor, and at the other extreme are the new élite of the high technology society with money to burn. It is strange that in such an enlightened age this can be allowed to happen. It is happening because organizations are ignoring the possibility of obsolescence, and refusing to prepare for the new skills of the future. Government, workers and employers are all at fault in not making the effort and the investment in training for the future.

People caught in this trap tend to sit back and wait hopefully for someone to do something. They could take action themselves and make sure they keep their skills up to date. The only way to avoid human obsolescence is by continuous training and development of human knowledge, skills, attitudes and behaviour.

Supporting people at work

People working in a world of constant change need to be supported at work. As much of the work that people do is computer based, part of the support needs to stem from the computer (see Chapter 5), but a large measure of the support needs to come from colleagues and supervisors. One approach I have come across in Australia is described below.

The need of people for support is fully recognised in this division of a large company. To meet the need the division have introduced a 'mentor' system. Each person selects someone that they would like to be their mentor. This person can be a colleague, or a supervisor. The role of mentors is to support the person in any way they can, not when they feel the need to intervene, but only when invited by the person they are mentoring. The approach is not new, but in this case it works well because mentors are not seen as supervisors, but as friends.

In the example above I think the approach would be much more powerful if the mentors were trained in counselling.

People should also get support and encouragement from their direct supervisors, not as mentors, but as supervisors. The primary role of supervisors is to help people to do their jobs in the best way possible, to help them to learn, and to encourage them in all aspects of their personal growth and development. Few of the supervisors I have met would either recognize that this was their role, or if they did, be able to carry it out. In a learning organization a primary activity would be to train all supervisors and managers in 'Helping People to Learn'. Unless these skills are available throughout the organization I don't think it is possible to support people in a beneficial way.

Successful change management

There are three major steps in successfully managing change within an organization. These are:

- monitor and plan for change
- welcome change
- equip people to adapt to change

Monitor and plan for change

This involves constantly reviewing the way the business enviroment is changing from all points of view, and then carefully defining the way in which the likely changes will affect the skills of people in the organization.

Once a picture forms then training plans have to be put in place to equip the people with the skills they need to adapt easily to the changes. This is easier said than done, but it is a task which should be given high priority.

Welcome change

Organizations should develop an attitude throughout, that change is a good thing. This will happen if they concentrate on becoming a learning organization, and if they equip their people with knowledge, skills, and attitudes to accept and adapt to change.

Equip people to adapt to change

Perhaps the only way that this can be done is by fostering a climate of constant change and development within the organization, with everyone encouraged to learn and grow, and by building really effective continuous training and support systems.

Key points

- Successful people and organizations display an ability to respond well to change.
- Creating a responsive workforce is virtually the same as building a learning organization.
- Learning is the process of discovery and acceptance of new experiences.
- Social change, organizational change, and technology change are the primary change agents.
- Particular job skills become obsolete.
- People need to be supported at work.
- Change management involves three steps:
  —planning for change;
  —welcoming change;
  —equipping people to adapt to change.

3 The psychology of training for success

People react in varying ways to change. If management want to train people to cope successfully with, and adapt to, change they have to deal with the psychological implications of change. This is particularly true of technology change, which most people approach with a degree of apprehension. By looking at the psychological implications of technology change it is possible to relate them to other forms of change.

Why should the prospect of technology change cause people to be apprehensive? I believe that it is partly because of the mystique which surrounds the use of computers, partly because of the feeling of not being in control, and partly because few, if any, systems have been designed to be easy to use.

People who understand the mystique, who have been initiated, and who have learned to control the machine quickly become 'systematized'. They have the effect of making everyone else feel positively useless. This feeling can be so strong that some people remove it by refusing to have anything to do with computers. People don't feel so bad about something that they have chosen not to do. For many people it is not possible to reject the computer in this way, and they have to face the prospect of learning to use the technology.

The prospect of learning something new causes apprehension because:

- people are dealing with something new and strange
- they feel inadequate and unprepared
- they don't know what to expect
- they have heard rumours about difficulties and problems

For some people this prospect may generate a feeling of being challenged, a feeling of excitement. For others anxiety may cause physical symptoms of illness. This will naturally depend on the individual's make-up and past experience and conditioning.

From a training point of view these problems have to be dealt with at the very outset, or the people concerned will never reach the stage where effective learning can take place. What then are the psychological barriers that have to be removed? There are, I believe, five critical psychological barriers, and this is true of all forms of change:

- fear of the unknown

- self-doubt, particularly in respect to the question 'Will I be able to cope?'
- fear of ridicule
- negative motivation
- fear of failure and censure

Fear of the unknown

All human beings fear the unknown, to varying degrees. This fear is based on anticipation that all might not be well, that there might be some disturbance to their comfort or security, both physical and mental. This feeling is evidenced by the comment many people make after experiencing something new, 'It wasn't as bad as I thought'.

Self-doubt

From the very beginning of their lives people are constantly given incorrect information about themselves. Much of this information is negative. People are told they are stupid, they are naughty, they look a mess, their hair needs cutting, and so on. This builds a strong negative attitude towards themselves. When people are faced with some kind of challenge all these negative thoughts surface, and they doubt their ability to cope.

Fear of ridicule

Everyone has a strong sense of belonging. This is reflected in the need people have to be accepted by a variety of peer groups. This acceptance is important to them, and to be accepted they have to be equal or similar to their peers. To be different generates ridicule, and could lead to rejection and isolation.

Negative motivation

To carry out any activity people need to be motivated. This motivation can be either positive, i.e. they want to do it, or negative, i.e. they don't want to do it, but they will to get it out of the way. When people are negatively motivated they do the minimum necessary and they learn very little, hoping they will never have to do it again.

Fear of failure and censure

Many people have learned that failure is a sign of weakness, and will lead to ridicule or worse. A very competitive educational environment increases the fear of failure and the consequent censure. Many people are, therefore, hesitant about trying new things in case they fail.

These five psychological barriers have to be removed if trainers are going to develop training which is enjoyable and effective. The first step in doing this is to recognize that the barriers exist and need to be removed. Removing the psychological barriers requires trainers to do three things:

- convert the unknown into the known
- encourage people to concentrate on their strengths
- develop positive motivation

The unknown becomes the known

This apparent contradiction is achieved by relating the new thing to be learned to something that the individual will already have experienced, and dealt with successfully, e.g. driving a car, using a telephone, using a washing machine. This approach softens the threat of the unknown and simplifies the concept of what has to be learned.

Concentrate on strengths

Everybody has strengths, things that they accept they are good at. By bringing these out into the open, and by showing how they are important, an atmosphere of confidence is created. This can be done very successfully by asking the people involved to state what they are good at, and then getting them to consider how these attributes can be used in learning the new thing.

Develop positive motivation

It is possible to generate positive attitudes towards learning by the simple process of examining all the reasons why people should not bother to learn the specific task. What happens is that by directing attention to the fact that it is OK to 'not want to do something', a strong positive feeling is generated to want to do it. This can be seen when children do the exact opposite of what they are told not to do.

Here is a case study of removing psychological barriers:

A large UK company was introducing a new computer-based sales order processing system. The existing system worked via telephone sales staff who rang the customer and took the order, entering the details onto an order form. The new system required the orders to be entered directly into the system via a keyboard. The company wanted to train the existing staff to use the new system. All the psychological barriers were in evidence in the following ways:

- The staff feared the unknown new system. They understood and were happy using the existing system.
- Everyone doubted their ability to work with the new system. Some of the staff had never even seen a computer terminal, let alone used one.
- Some of the older, highly skilled, staff felt that the new system would mean a loss of status for them.
- None of the staff saw any convincing reason for the introduction of the new system.

These barriers were removed in the following way:

- The staff were asked whether they could operate a television, an adding machine, and a typewriter. They all could. They were then shown the computer terminal which was a combination of all three. Next they were asked how fast did they think they could input data via the keyboard. They decided that the speed depended upon the speed that the customer gave them the order. So they didn't need to learn to type, especially as most of the input was numerical.
- The staff were asked what they were good at. The general answer was 'telephone selling'. The importance of telephone selling was emphasized and the technology was described as a new way of taking orders that would help them to sell more. As the staff were paid sales commission this became an encouragement.

- The final step was to offer the staff the choice of continuing to use the paperbased system, with other staff inputting the data into the system. They quickly recognized that this would not enable them to use the features of the new system that would help them to sell more, and so they chose to use the new system.

The net result was that the staff became very positively motivated to learn the new system, and did so very successfully.

Learning to do new things should be and can be fun. When the psychological barriers have been removed trainers can concentrate on making the training programme very enjoyable. To do this they have to know what people enjoy, particularly in relation to a learning experience. This will vary from person to person, but there are three key factors that make learning enjoyable and effective. These are:

- an opportunity to choose what and how to learn
- an opportunity to experiment
- an opportunity to self-monitor the learning

These opportunities can be provided by creating a training programme that is based on learning-centred design principles (see Chapter 10). For technology change trainers can make use of the technology in an imaginative way. For example, the learners are introduced to the computer terminal, and then allowed to decide how they want to go about learning. The programme should offer them the choice of recording or not recording their activities, and a choice of how they want to proceed through the programme. The emphasis should be placed on the ease and fun of using the technology to learn.

One of the problems that the trainer will encounter in approaching technology training in this way is that system designers are still not recognizing the psychological implications of the interface between people and machines.

Technology design for people means building systems that are easy to use, and easy to learn. This means giving a great deal of thought to the way information is presented via the computer screen, and the language that is used. For example, one idea I have recently introduced is to eliminate all error messages from computer systems, especially the cryptic type, e.g. 'E006 MANDATORY NUMERIC FIELD'. These are replaced with ACTION messages which are up to three lines long and which explain the correct way to carry out the task, rather than what has gone wrong. This approach is more acceptable to users, and reinforces their learning.

Trainers should do whatever they can to simplify what has to be learned, and to relate it as closely as possible to people's existing knowledge and experiences. The closer people can relate to whatever is being learned, then the fewer and less difficult will be the psychological barriers that trainers have to overcome.

Key points

- Learning something new causes apprehension because:
  —it is new and strange;

—people feel inadequate and unprepared;
—they don't know what to expect;
—there are always rumours about difficulties.

- There are five critical psychological barriers to all forms of change;
  —fear of the unknown;
  —self-doubt;
  —fear of ridicule;
  —negative motivation; and
  —fear of failure and censure.
- Removing these barriers can be done by:
  —converting the unknown into the known;
  —encouraging people to concentrate on their strengths; and
  —developing positive motivation.
- Learning can be made enjoyable and effective by providing:
  —an opportunity to choose what and how to learn;
  —an opportunity to experiment; and
  —an opportunity to self-monitor learning.

PART TWO

The business of training

4 The strategic role of training

Any organization that wants to succeed, and continue to succeed, has to recruit and maintain a workforce consisting of people who are willing to accept change and willing to learn and develop continuously. This is true of everyone in the workforce from the chief executive to the newest recruit.

Training and developing human potential is so important in the effective management of change, and in the maintenance of a skilled workforce, that it has to be a main board responsibility. Whether the person is called Human Resources Director, Personnel Director, Training Director, or People Director matters little, so long as the person exists and is given the budget necessary to do the job.

The job of the People Director can be divided into three main parts:

- defining and monitoring the people skills needed;
- recruiting people capable of meeting or of developing to meet these needs; and
- providing the learning opportunities and resources needed by the people.

Defining and monitoring people needs

This task has been variously described as manpower planning, human resource assessment, and skill needs analysis. Once again it is not the name given to the activity that matters, it is the work that is done to identify the corporate needs at all levels that is important. This is not a one-off exercise—it is a continuous process of assessing business needs as they constantly change.

The starting point for this assessment of needs will be the corporate strategic plan, and how management anticipate the plan is going to be achieved. As the corporate strategic plan can only be achieved by people it is obviously a first priority to ensure that the appropriate people exist and have the appropriate skills. So the first step is to define what these needs are.

Recruiting the people needed

As the workforce is never static there will always be a need to recruit people. This process, just as the monitoring of people needs, is a continuous one. It requires the preparation of appropriate recruitment policies and procedures. These will include the levels at which recruitment will take place, and the ways that recruitment will be carried out. Bringing in people of the desired calibre is very important as all subsequent development will depend on the basic knowledge, skills, attitudes, and behaviour that recruits bring with them.

Learning opportunities and resources

I believe that training can be defined as 'helping people to learn'. This means that the primary role of training is to create and provide the very best learning opportunities and resources. This should apply at all times during normal work (on the job), and on specific occasions organized to help people to learn (off the job). I distinguish between 'on the job', and 'off the job', purely to relate what follows to current thinking. Unfortunately this separation has only served to suggest that 'the job' is different from training, i.e. that 'off the job' training is not part of 'the job'.

If a job is seen as including thinking about, learning about, and doing a prescribed set of activities, then people can both think about, and learn about the job either when doing it, or when not doing it, but it is still all part of the job.

This leads to the thought that the separation between 'on the job' and 'off the job' training is pointless, and only serves to make the learning done 'off the job' appear less productive than the learning done 'on the job'. This couldn't be further from the truth.

Learning is something people choose to do when they are interested in what is happening around them. If the environment in which people work is also one in which they can learn, then people will have the opportunity to develop and maintain the skills they need.

The learning organization

Learning involves a constant interaction between people and their environment through experimentation, exploration, and questioning. An environment that is exciting, and one in which people have fun, leads to considerable learning and growth. Building a learning organization means encouraging people to be themselves, to question and explore their working environment, and to be able to influence what goes on around them. For this to happen changes have to take place in what I will call the conventional rule-based organization, where supervision is concerned with getting people to toe the line rather than learn and grow. To learn, people have to open their minds to new ideas and suggestions, and this is encouraged in the learning organization.

In the learning organization training is not an activity which is separate from day to day activities: it is an inherent part of the working environment. When a person needs to know something, or wants to learn something, the information and the facilities to learn should be immediately available to them. Sometimes this can be done while the work activity continues, and sometimes a short break may need to be taken. Where it is not possible for the work activity to be interrupted people should be able to access training as soon as they can. People should be encouraged to take the time and make the effort to learn, and this encouragement should come from colleagues, supervisors, and management.

The learning organization is willing to learn from customers, from suppliers, from competitors, from the market place, and from its workforce. In this way change is not only accepted, it is eagerly sought out, and the challenge it brings is welcomed. This reduces the impact of change, and strengthens the organization's ability to be flexible.

Developing a learning culture

A learning culture grows from practice and example. When senior management act in a way which shows the people who work for them that they are willing to listen and learn, and that they believe in constant and continuous attention to the learning needs of others, then people will model their own attitudes accordingly. There is no way that a new approach can be 'announced'. It has to be introduced slowly and carefully, starting with the chief executive.

Here is an example of a consultancy assignment with a company in the USA:

The president of the company had recognized what he saw as a serious problem when visiting an operating unit of the company. This had been supported by an increase in customer complaints. I was asked to help. The first task was to discover what the current situation was with regard to the apparent lack of competence. A study was carried out and I reported the findings to the project team as follows:

- on the job training was a joke;
- the average off the job training was three days per person per annum;
- training courses and materials were old-fashioned, highly directive, and 'to be avoided';
- the training budget was reasonable, but not being used very well;
- managers did not recognize the potential value and importance of training, but perhaps this was in response to the current quality of training;
- good performance was not related to good training in the eyes of the management;
- job descriptions existed but did not include the desired competency levels.

The team, which included the senior training manager took the report to the president, who wanted to know who to blame.

My next meeting with him was hard going. 'Well,' he said, 'if this report is to be believed, someone is going to pay, and I want to know who it is.' He didn't like my answer: 'What do you mean, I am,' he shouted. 'Why me?' 'Well as head of the company for the last ten years you have let this happen', was my response. I hurried to add that I thought we should look forward, and start to put things right.

'Good idea', he sighed, 'what do you suggest?' I ventured that perhaps we could begin by creating a 'learning environment' throughout the entire company. Making the company into a 'learning organization'. One that was keen to learn, grow, and develop, and give its people the space and time to learn, grow, and develop into the best team in the business. 'So where do we start?' I explained that the only place was at the very top. I suggested that he and his colleagues must have a lot to learn, if the company had got into such a mess, and anyway wouldn't it set a good example if we started at the top. If top management were prepared to admit that they had things to learn then others would do the same.

The programme involved five related elements:

- a general awareness programme, 'Learning for Growth';

- a 'Performance Impact Review', relating individual performance to the success (profitability) of the business;
- the establishing of 'Competency Targets';
- a series of courses for management, 'Helping People to Learn';
- and last but not least, a complete overhaul of training, and the development of a 'Learning-Centred Approach'.

The problem is well on the way to being put right, and the organization is growing a learning culture.

Performance and profits

The link between the performance of people and profits is generally accepted as being obvious. However, when individuals are asked how their performance impacts on profits they are often hard pressed to produce a direct link. The link can be established for every member of the workforce (see Chapter 6). Once this link is established it is possible to measure how improved performance will increase profit.

If improved performance comes from the growth and development of individual skills, then a direct link can be made between training and profits. Helping people to learn is directly helping to improve performance, and hence profits. The investment that is made in training may not have an immediate payoff, but then few investments have. By measuring the returns from training in terms of performance improvement it is possible to prepare financial investment appraisals for training initiatives (see Chapter 6). This provides management with a clear indication of the value of the training investment and helps to convince everyone that training is a valuable investment in people.

Investing in the future

The future success of the business is forged today. It is forged on the anvil of experience by the craft of skilled trainers and their management colleagues. Everything that individuals do both 'on the job' and 'off the job' should lead them to learn something about themselves, and about what they are doing. Learning opportunities should be sought out by everyone. People should be encouraged to explore areas that interest them, and to grow and develop as people, whether or not what they are learning has an immediate connection with the work they are doing.

A programme was started in a UK company to provide staff with the opportunity to learn another language. The aim was to provide a learning centre with language courses so that staff could spend time during lunch hours and in the evening learning the language of their choice. The programme was publicized on the basis of people being able to enjoy their overseas holidays, and have the satisfaction of speaking another language. The programme was a great success, and when the company opened an office in France it was able to send several of the 'French speaking' staff over to run the office.

It is not easy for an organization to provide facilities that are not 'job' related. There seems to be an attitude that only learning directly concerned with the 'job' is valid, and that any other learning is inappropriate. This attitude is very backward thinking.

When management are thinking about the future they cannot possibly know what individuals will aspire to do, so they cannot assume that current learning is not valid for the future simply because it doesn't relate to the 'current job'. If management are truly concerned to equip people for the future then they have to take a forward-looking attitude, and support and encourage people to learn the things they want to learn, as well as the things that link in with the company's strategic plan.

Strategies for success

Success is measured in a wide variety of ways. Corporate success is usually measured on the basis of profitability, but there are always other factors involved such as high quality, efficient and friendly service, and so on. Individuals measure success differently. Some clearly measure success in terms of their income, and display their success through status symbols. Others measure success in terms of personal achievement, e.g. learning to speak another language, being able to make good presentations, being elected as captain of the golf club, and so on. So in developing strategies for success it is first necessary to decide what constitutes success. Here is an example of a success statement.

We will consider that we are successful if we earn profit per person of $50000, and if we see a reduction in the number of customer complaints to less than 100 per year, if our accident-free operating days reach the 2000 target, and if we all achieve our personal success statements.

The organization can issue regular bulletins of how close they are to these success targets. At the individual level everyone should prepare their own success statement, which is agreed with their manager, and which is used as a basis for measuring progress. It is valuable if personal success statements include some items that relate to performance, and to helping to achieve the corporate success criteria. Once this approach is in place it becomes possible to determine the appropriate strategies at the personal and the corporate level.

If every member of the workforce is interested in and committed to personal performance and achieving their own success criteria, then there is every chance that the corporate criteria can be achieved. Setting corporate targets without every individual knowing how they can contribute is doomed to failure.

Corporate success depends upon individual success. Individual success depends upon the motivation and support individuals receive to learn, to grow, and to improve performance.

Key points

- Training and developing human potential is a critical strategic activity.
- There are three key tasks involved:
  —defining and monitoring the people skills needed;
  —recruiting people capable of meeting or of developing to meet these needs; and
  —providing the learning opportunities and resources needed.
- Learning is something people do when they are interested in what is going on around them.
- The learning organization is one that ensures that learning takes place by providing constant interaction between people and their environment through experimentation, exploration, and questioning.

- In the learning organization training is part of the working environment.
- A learning culture grows from practice and example.
- Improved performance equals increased profits.
- Building a learning organization improves performance.
- Corporate success depends upon individual success.

5 Developing a training strategy for the future

The emphasis throughout this book is on preparing for a future of constant change by making an effective investment in people, through designing and delivering learning-centred training, and by using the best possible tools and techniques. This calls for the creation of a coherent training strategy for the future.

But what should such a strategy cover, and how can it be built? These are two questions which need to be answered before an appropriate strategy can be developed.

Perhaps it would be useful to start by defining what is meant by the word 'strategy'. This word, now very popular in business circles, is concerned with the process of planning and preparation, so as to put oneself in the best possible position to deal with future events. It was originally used to describe the process by which generals manipulated their forces to ensure that they were always in a position to deal with the enemy from the most advantageous position possible.

A 'strategy' can be seen as *a plan for utilising resources in the best possible way, to meet defined, or anticipated needs in the future.* The starting point for developing such a strategy would seem to be a clear definition of learning needs, followed by an indication of the training programmes and products required to meet the needs, and finally an idea of the resources needed to produce the training required.

Learning-needs analysis

In Chapter 6 the idea of carrying out a training audit is examined. This is the starting point for the learning-needs analysis which flows naturally from the training audit and seeks to identify, for various sections and groupings of employees, the gap between the current levels of knowledge, skill, attitude and behaviour, and those which are needed.

The process of training, i.e. helping people to learn, is really a process of helping people to move from their 'present position' to a 'desired position', which enables them to improve their performance. This movement can be described as a journey through a 'learning domain'. The learners undertake the journey from their 'present position', and cross a 'learning terrain' to reach their 'desired position'. The path they follow on this journey can be called the 'learning path'. This 'learning process' can be depicted in the form of a simple diagram (see Figure 5.1).

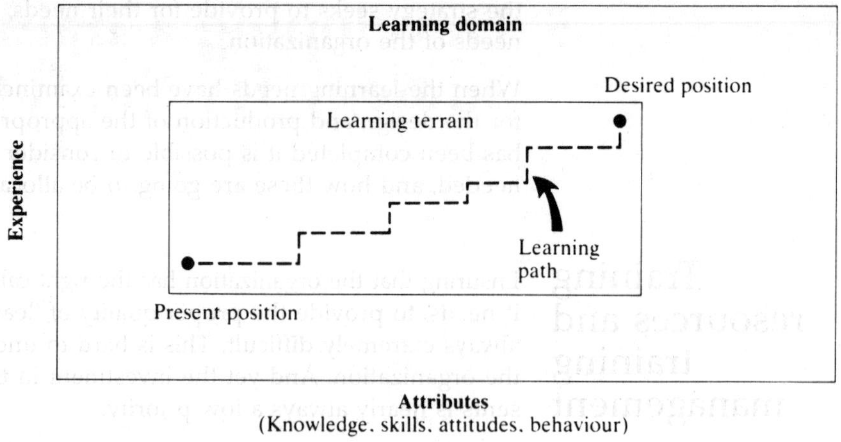

Figure 5.1 *The learning process*

Before it is realistic to develop the strategy, the 'learning domain', the 'learning terrain', and the 'learning path' for every individual must be defined. In the past, it was thought that this required highly skilled analysts with the ability to interview people and assess their answers. The task was time consuming and complex. Today the use of 'expert' systems can make the task more straightforward, with people answering questions posed by a computer within a pre-defined structure. The system can in turn respond to the vagaries of the answers given.

Once the learning-needs analysis has been completed, using human 'experts', or 'expert' machines, the work can start on creating the training programmes and products needed.

Training programmes and products

Providing training materials is always difficult; without knowing the needs of the organization and its people it is impossible. Learning-centred design is the recommended philosophy to follow, and is the basis of the Advanced Training Methodology, which is used to design and build the training programmes and products that are required.

Throughout this book I am concerned that training is seen as the process of *helping people to learn*. This is very important because the training strategy being constructed is really a 'facilitation of learning' strategy. For this to succeed it has to be known (a) what the organization wants people to learn, and (b) what the people themselves want to learn. The training programmes and products produced are designed and built to ensure, as far as one can ever do, that this learning takes place. Perhaps this is better described as providing the very best learning opportunities.

Unfortunately a great many training programmes and products are concerned with delivering a particular message, and giving a particular knowledge or skill. In doing so they give scant regard to what the learner may want to learn, or be motivated to learn. In any strategy being built it is essential to ensure that learners are put first, and that the strategy seeks to provide for their needs, and by so doing meets the needs of the organization.

When the learning needs have been examined, and a coherent schedule for the design and production of the appropriate 'learning opportunities' has been completed it is possible to consider the resources that are needed, and how these are going to be allocated and managed.

Training resources and training management

Ensuring that the organization has the right calibre and number of trainers it needs, to provide the proper quality of 'learning opportunities', is always extremely difficult. This is hard to understand. The people *are* the organization. And yet the investment in people that training represents is nearly always a low priority.

If we see the role of training as *'ensuring that the organization has the people with the correct mix of attributes, through providing appropriate learning opportunities, and motivating people to learn, and thus enabling them to perform to the highest levels of quality and service'* then it is obvious that the role is of paramount importance.

Training must therefore be managed as a front-line business activity. It requires a wide understanding of business in general, the organization, and the needs of its people. It also requires a clear understanding of how the knowledge, skill, attitudes, and behaviour, i.e. the attributes of its people, can be harnessed for the benefit of the organization.

Once the learning needs have been identified, the programmes and products specified, and resources determined (no mean achievement), it must be made to happen.

The corporate training strategy

The corporate training strategy should be presented in a detailed document that contains the following elements:

- The training audit.
- Learning-needs analysis.
- The training approach (programmes and products).
- The management of learning.
- The training investment.

In addition to this strategy document every individual in the organization should have a 'learning plan'. These plans should be a part of the overall strategy, and enable detailed planning of the likely demand for, and use of, the training programmes and products.

The training strategy would probably have three levels, short term (this year), medium term (next year), long term (three–five years). The short term would deal with the most immediate needs, some of which could be to deal with current problems. The medium term would look at the enhancement of specific attributes, needed to meet performance targets, and the long term would look at personal and corporate growth.

Implementing the training strategy

There are a variety of ways that the training strategy can be implemented. Whichever way is followed the responsibilities for the different aspects of training remain unchanged. There are three levels of responsibility:

- management
- training
- learners

Management

Managers are responsible for seeing that their people perform well. This clearly implies that they are responsible for the continuous training and support of their people, which covers recognizing needs, providing the time and encouragement, and paying the bills.

Training

The training group are responsible for providing the very best learning opportunities for the people whose needs have been recognized by management, or articulated by the individuals themselves.

Learners

Learners are totally responsible for their own learning. They meet this responsibility by utilizing the learning opportunities provided for them by training.

These responsibilities can be fully met in all kinds of different ways. I will discuss the three main approaches to implementing the training strategy, which are:

- centralized
- de-centralized
- distributed

Centralized

A centralized approach to introducing the training strategy involves a central training unit receiving requests from management to meet their training needs. The central training unit provides resources, all based on learning-centred design (see Chapter 10), which are delivered either centrally or locally. All training staff report to the central unit, and participate directly in the delivery of the training.

Training resources in a 'distance learning' format are prepared centrally, but used locally. Training policy and approach are decided centrally and management have to process all their training requirements via the central unit.

This approach enables the consistency and quality of training to be controlled, and ensures that all training is designed and produced using the appropriate methodologies, and following the learning-centred design philosophy.

De-centralized

This is the opposite approach to the centralized one, and places training units in the local sites, reporting to local management. Local needs are met directly, and the local training units are able to provide resources, or obtain them externally to meet local needs.

There can be a central policy unit agreeing strategy and coordinating the local training efforts, or the local training units may be given full autonomy.

I came across a very good example of the de-centralized approach in a large UK company, where each subsidiary had its own training manager, and where there was a centrally-based training coordinator. They held two training conferences each year at which the overall policy and direction of training were discussed, and information and ideas shared. There was a good rapport and the training managers were very comfortable with local autonomy, but with a recognition of the need for an overall policy and strategy.

Standards have to be maintained in the de-centralized environment and this is, of course, more difficult than in the centralized approach. There is also a risk of effort being duplicated, and of local training units deviating from the desired direction. On the other hand the local needs of the organization can be more appropriately met.

Distributed

This approach is really a combination of the two previous approaches. It works on the basis of having a centrally-based unit to provide training resources, which are consistent and of high quality. These resources are delivered locally by training managers responsible to local management.

The local management decide what training they need, and the local training manager then provides it, either from the central training unit, or from outside. This approach seems to bring together the advantages of both the centralized and de-centralized approaches, and is the one I prefer. However, all three approaches can work very well provided there is a strong and well-thought-out strategy in the first place.

Corporate training strategy is the key to the building of a truly 'learning organization' and thereby future prosperity. If organizations want a highly motivated, up-to-date, creative, and productive workforce, they need to start now and build a strategy for the future. This strategy has to recognize that corporate performance is totally dependent upon the performance of the organization's people. This then leads to a clear commitment to invest in these people through training, while appreciating that people only learn what they want to learn.

The strategy must therefore deal with how people's learning desire can be stimulated and fed by learning-centred designed training, and how performance is going to be measured, and competences assessed. There are no easy answers, and the rapidly changing working environment of the future is not going to get any easier. A start has to be made now to develop the strategies that will make the organization well prepared for the future.

Key points

- A strategy is a plan for utilizing resources in the best possible way to meet defined or anticipated future needs.
- Developing a training strategy involves a comprehensive learning-needs analysis.
- Training is helping people to learn.
- The training strategy is really a 'facilitation of learning' strategy.
- Such a strategy must cover:
  —what the organization wants people to learn, and
  —what the people themselves want to learn.

- **The role of training is: ensuring that the organization has the people with the correct mix of attributes through providing learning opportunities and motivating people to learn, and thus enabling them to perform to the highest levels of quality and service.**
- **Training must be managed as a front-line business activity.**
- **The training strategy document should contain:**
  —the training audit;
  —the learning-needs analysis;
  —the training approach (programmes and products);
  —the management of learning approach; and
  —the training investment.
- **Individuals should have their own learning plans.**
- **Managers are responsible for seeing that their people perform well.**
- **Trainers are responsible for providing the best learning opportunities.**
- **Learners are totally responsible for their own learning.**
- **The training strategy can be implemented in one of three ways:**
  —centralized;
  —de-centralized; or
  —distributed.

6 Training—an investment for success

The investment in people, both in developing and maintaining the appropriate skills, becomes a vital part of the organization's strategy for the future. Although there may be fewer people employed in traditional manual and semi-skilled roles, the people who operate computers, and thereby control the activities of the business, create a new form of dependence. There is at the present time a shortage of people with these important skills and this is only likely to grow, unless there is a change in attitudes towards training and an increase in the investment in people.

Unfortunately training is frequently seen as a cost, an expense rather than an investment. The amount that most organizations invest in their people via training seems little more than a token gesture, taking a tiny fraction of the corporate income. Why should this be so? Noone knows the answer to this question, but one contributory factor is that many managers cannot see the link between training and profit. They understand that training improves people, but cannot relate this improvement directly with profit. This is made worse by trainers who cannot demonstrate the direct and significant impact that training has on profits. In fact many trainers play down this aspect of their work.

Like any investment, investment in training should produce an effective and measurable payback. If it doesn't, or if the payback cannot be quantified in terms of profit, then there is something wrong, or someone hasn't done their homework.

Effective training enhances the knowledge, skills, attitudes and behaviour of the people, and hence their performance. The improved performance of individuals leads directly to profit. Such a payback can be rapid and significant, yet it is rarely measured or presented in financial terms.

Investments in capital equipment have, for many years, been appraised by the use of well-established financial techniques. These same techniques are rarely, if ever, used for the appraisal of training investment. This is a shame because they are ideal for showing how training investment can produce rapid and exciting returns.

Money can be used in two ways; it can be spent, or it can be invested. Spending provides the satisfaction of some immediate need. Investment provides the satisfaction of some future return. Training by its very nature creates future benefits, both for the individual and for the company; it must therefore be an investment. But it is nearly always seen and accounted for as spending. I believe there are three key aspects of evaluating training in terms of profit. These are: determining costs and benefits; training investment appraisal; and training audit.

Determining costs and benefits

In carrying out an investment appraisal two key elements have to be quantified, the value and duration of the investment, and the value and duration of the benefits received. The investment usually takes place before benefits are received so there is a time lag. This can be depicted as a graph (see Figure 6.1).

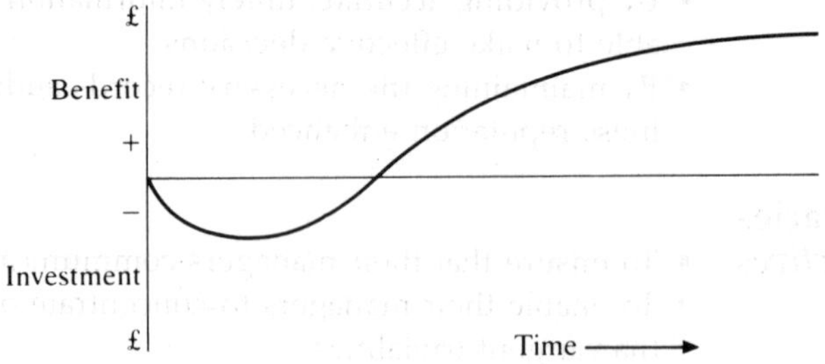

Figure 6.1 *Investment payback curve*

Because the benefits are received in the future an estimate of the value has to be made. Such estimates are always difficult for any kind of investment, so trainers should not be put off by the difficulty of calculating such future benefits.

If this form of investment appraisal were completed for training projects, management would take a much more positive attitude to training investment, and would perhaps stop seeing training as an expense.

All good training produces benefits. The job of the trainer is to identify clearly and quantify the benefits, and then to present them to management in an effective and acceptable way. This gives rise to the problem of identifying and quantifying benefits. It is not normally difficult to place a value on the investment; it is usually possible to work out what things will cost.

To quantify training benefits it is necessary to know how the improvement of individual performance affects profit. Profit is the surplus remaining after deducting the cost of resources consumed from the income generated by the business. Profits can be increased by improving the quality and quantity of sales, i.e. increased income, or by reducing the quantity or value of the resources consumed, i.e. costs.

Improvement in the individual's performance must impact on one or all of these areas. Once the area of impact has been identified for every employee, it becomes possible to measure the effect of training on profit. It might be argued that the impact on profit of every employee cannot be identified. However every employee must have an impact on profit, even if it is only the cost of their salary, and it should always be possible to state the reason for incurring that cost. It can be shown how the impact on profit can be valued by taking examples for accountants, secretaries, production workers, drivers and salesmen.

Accountants

Primary objectives

- To manage the business funds
- To provide information for management
- To maintain accounting records

Impact on profits

- By controlling funds effectively loans are kept to a minimum and interest is saved
- By providing accurate, timely information, management are better able to make effective decisions
- By maintaining the necessary records audit fees are reduced, and business reputation enhanced

Secretaries

Primary objectives

- To ensure that their managers communicate effectively
- To enable their managers to concentrate on important priorities rather than urgent trivialities

Impact on profits

- By ensuring that managers are efficient and effective they can directly improve management productivity, and by being efficient themselves, administration costs are reduced

Production workers

Primary objectives

- To produce *X* quantity of *Y* within a specified time, to the specified level of quality, using the minimum specified materials

Impact on profits

- Less rejects
- Less material waste
- More output

Drivers

Primary objectives

- To deliver the goods to the customer when and where required
- To drive carefully and economically
- To be courteous and helpful

Impact on profits

- Repeat business is maintained by the efficiency and quality of the service given
- Delivery costs are reduced

Salesmen

Primary objectives

- To persuade existing customers to buy more
- To get new customers

Impact on profits

- Quantity of sales at the best possible prices is increased
- Quality of customers is improved

From this brief list it can be seen that it is possible to clarify the primary objectives for all employees, and then link these to the impact they have on profits. Depending on the type and size of business the impact of individuals will of course vary, and not necessarily in relation to their costs. By carrying out an exercise for the whole business it is possible to identify those people where improved performance through training is likely to have the greatest impact on profit. To do this it is necessary to measure the impact in financial terms. Taking one example from the list, accountants, the value of training can be calculated on just one aspect of their job: the funds management aspect.

Here is some basic information about the funds of the business:

Overdraft	£1 500 000	
Debtors	£2 200 000	(they take 100 days to pay)
Creditors	£1 400 000	(the business takes 40 days to pay)

If the accountant can reduce the time debtors take to pay, the balance outstanding will reduce, and thus reduce the overdraft. If the time is reduced by 20 days it will reduce by £440 000 (£22 000 per day x 20 days). If the bank is being paid 12 per cent interest on the overdraft this will create a saving of *£52 800.*

If in addition the accountant can extend the time taken to pay creditors more will be borrowed from them instead of from the bank, so reducing the overdraft. If the time is extended by ten days it will increase creditors by £350 000 (£35 000 per day). This generates a further saving in interest of *£42 000.*

This potential impact on profit of *£94 000* makes it well worth while investing in training the accountant in 'effective funds management'. Please note that it is no use investing in better equipment or systems until the accountant is suitably trained to use them effectively.

This form of exercise can, and should, be carried out for every employee. It is easier to do for some than it is for others. Carrying out a performance audit in this way is an essential first step in a full training audit of the business which will identify:

- Where training can produce the greatest benefits.
- Where present training activities are ineffective.
- The extent and use of the training budget.
- How the training budget can be re-directed to greater effect.
- Where the training budget should be increased to reap the rewards from unharvested fields.

The ability to appraise the investment in training properly, and to stop treating the training budget as spending, is an essential first step in convincing management that training is a vital ingredient for corporate success.

Here is an example of a training investment appraisal. The example is in three sections. Section one briefly describes the training project. Section two defines the key elements, and section three (Figure 6.2) shows how the information can be presented.

Training investment appraisal

The training project

To produce a two-part training programme for company representatives to learn how to make better sales presentations, including the use of a demonstration video. The programme consisted of a talk given by a sales manager using pre-pared visuals including the video followed by example role playing. The training would be spread over three days and all salesmen would be trained in groups of five. It would take six months to complete the training programme.

The key elements

To prepare an investment appraisal the investment had to be valued, as did the benefits:

			£
The investment:	Item1	Production of video	23 000
	Item 2	Script and visuals	9 000
	Item 3	Salesmen's time 3 days × 80 salesmen = 240 days × £100* = £24 000 × 20%** =	4 800
			£36 800

*Average daily sales lost through training.
**20% is the contribution (gross profit) on sales.

The benefits: It was estimated that after the training the average daily sales figure would increase to £120. An increase of £20 per sales day:

80 salesmen x 180 sales days x £20 = £288 000

The contribution (gross profit) on sales was 20 per cent, so 20 per cent of £288 000 = *£57 600.*

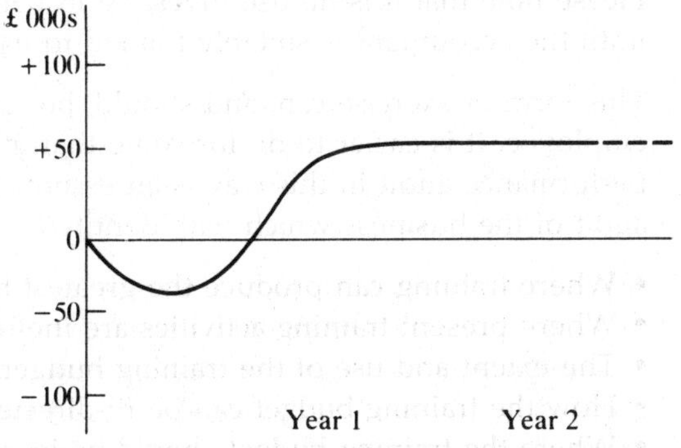

Figure 6.2 *Example investment appraisal*

In the above example the investment of £36 800 would be fully paid back in less than a year, and the annual savings would continue.

There is another very important point to consider when appraising the investment in training, particularly when comparing different approaches to the training. It is not sufficient simply to compare the 'up front' investment of each approach. The full 'life cycle' of the investment has to be examined.

Life-cycle investment analysis involves looking at every aspect of the investment, not just the preparation/purchase price. This will include such items as:

- training time
- running expenses
- travelling expenses
- maintenance expenses
- failure rates

The life-cycle investment approach makes comparisons between alternative approaches both realistic and practical. It also reveals the hidden investment that is often made in poor, cheap and ineffective training programmes. The concept can be depicted, as in Figure 6.3, as an iceberg where the bulk of the iceberg represents the full life-cycle cost of a project. Normally only the tip is visible, i.e. the immediate starting costs, with the bulk, i.e. the future costs, being hidden below the surface.

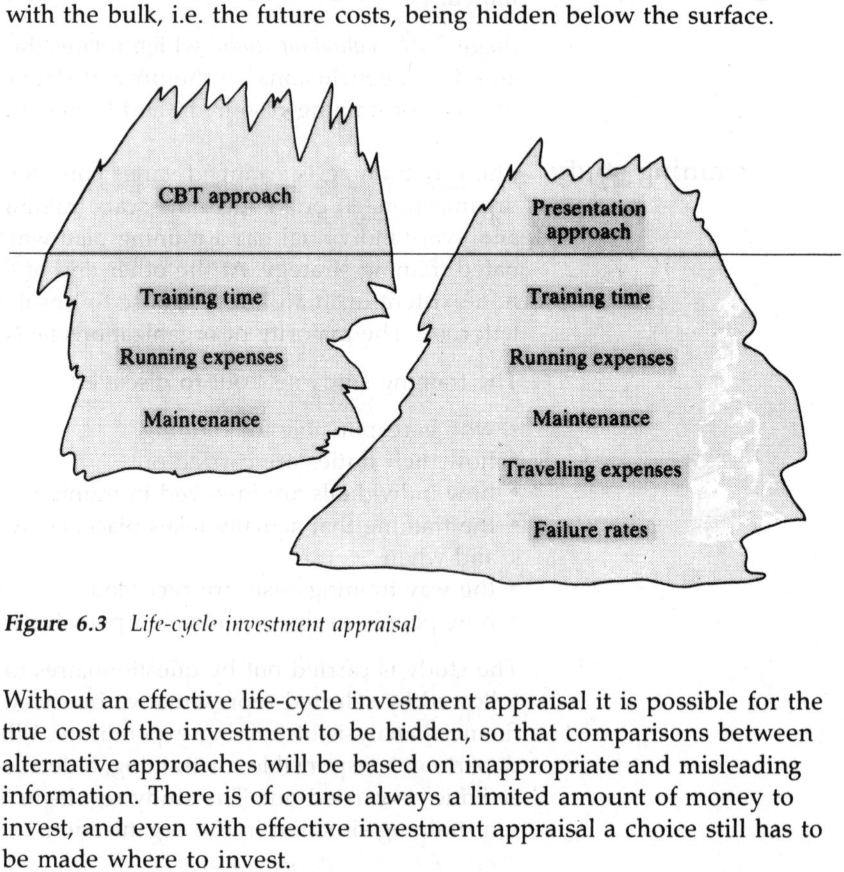

Figure 6.3 *Life-cycle investment appraisal*

Without an effective life-cycle investment appraisal it is possible for the true cost of the investment to be hidden, so that comparisons between alternative approaches will be based on inappropriate and misleading information. There is of course always a limited amount of money to invest, and even with effective investment appraisal a choice still has to be made where to invest.

Training audit

A training audit is a procedure for establishing the current situation in respect to the corporate investment in training, and then determining the potential for making the investment more effective.

The training audit is concerned with answering five key questions:

1 What is the current level of the investment in training?

2 Where is the investment directed?
3 Where could training produce the greatest benefits?
4 How can the training budget be re-directed?
5 Where should the training budget be increased?

The audit is carried out in three stages:

Stage 1 *A training study,* which analyses all training carried out at the present time with emphasis on its purpose. The study will also examine the systems and methods used for managing, monitoring and controlling the training budget.

Stage 2 *A performance study,* which looks at the work of every individual (or where appropriate, groups of people) and seeks to determine the impact their performance has on profits. Measuring current levels of performance is important so that degrees of improvement can be determined.

Stage 3 *An evaluation study,* which relates the first two studies together, and draws conclusions on the present state of affairs, pointing to areas of waste of training resources, and to neglected performance areas.

Training study

The way training is arranged varies considerably from organization to organization. At one end of the scale training is given a high priority, and every individual has a training plan which is part of a fully coordinated training strategy. At the other end of the scale training is either non-existent or in ad hoc response to unsolicited leaflets through the letterbox. The majority of organizations lie somewhere in between.

The training study sets out to discover:

- who is responsible for training
- how their duties are carried out
- how individuals are involved in training
- the training that actually takes place, i.e. who receives what training and when
- the way training costs are recorded
- how people in the organization perceive training

The study is carried out by questionnaires to employees and managers, followed by selected representative interviews. This is supported by a financial analysis of training expenditure. Where there is a person or department responsible for training, a detailed study of their work and activities is carried out. The study results in a report covering the current training situation in the organization.

Performance study

This is a difficult and often time-consuming exercise, but one that can bring enormous benefits. If all organizations made sure that every employee had their own objectives and impact statement, then it would be a straightforward task to link training with profitable performance. Unfortunately this is extremely rare. The first aim of the performance study is, therefore, to create these statements, starting with the chief executive. An example of an objectives/impact statement is given in Figure 6.4.

Objectives and Impact Statement
My Objectives are: • To produce specified work on time • To use materials efficiently • To look after my machine • To put forward ideas on how improvements can be made
The Impact I have on profit: • Improved quality products create customer satisfaction and loyalty • Reduced rejects • Reduced material waste • Lower costs through productivity
Name:

Figure 6.4 *Pocket-sized objectives/impact statement*

Once such statements exist it is possible to analyse the key performance areas and to assess the extent to which training could improve performance. At this point it is usual to encounter improvement barriers. These tend to consist of equipment, facilities and people that get in the way of obtaining better results from other people, particularly where performance could be improved by training.

An example might be a production worker who by improved knowledge and skill in handling materials could create less waste, but who does not have the necessary handling equipment to use the knowledge and skill. Performance barriers have to be removed before the training is going to be effective.

The performance study will, therefore, produce a report containing individual objective/impact statement; key performance areas; critical performance barriers; and performance-measuring devices.

Evaluation study

The evaluation study brings the two preceding studies together, compares what is actually happening with what needs to happen, and draws the appropriate conclusions. This phase can be depicted as two overlapping circles (see Figure 6.5).

The aim of the evaluation study is to increase the degree of overlap, and to make suggestions for re-directing the training budget to match the most important key performance areas. The evaluation study will, therefore, concentrate on identifying:

1 neglected key performance areas,
2 wasted training,
3 training effort that should be retained.

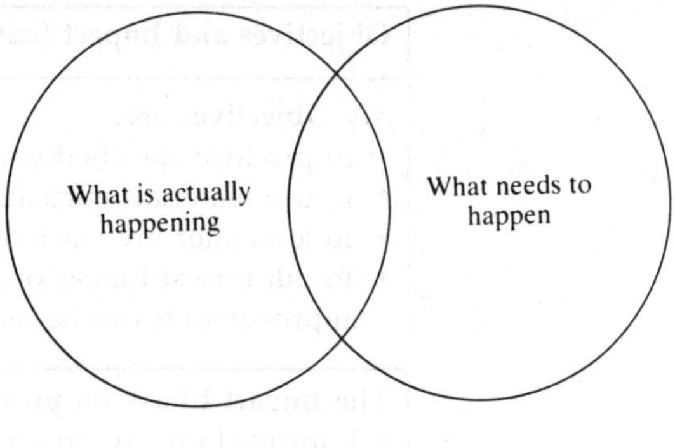

Figure 6.5 *Training effectiveness*

It is important that these three areas are identified and confirmed by management.

Neglected key performance areas are those areas where the impact on profit can be clearly seen and which are not receiving effective training.

Wasted training is training which, though it might be beneficial to the individual, does not attack key performance areas, or cannot be seen to have an impact on profit. Many trainers believe that no training is wasted, and in effect this is probably true if the view taken is broad enough. But what is of primary concern here is a profitable return on the training investment, and in this context a great deal of training is misdirected, or wasted.

Of course there will be much training effort that is properly directed and this must be retained and built into the training strategy.

The training audit will finally present a financial statement that will show firstly the level of the present investment and its returns, and secondly the suggested level of investment and the potential returns. The three parts of the audit, the training study, the performance study, and the evaluation study, lead in turn to the financial assessment of the training investment.

The training audit report is a far-reaching document that places a totally new perspective on the approach to training in the organization and leads directly to the need for developing a coherent training strategy. This strategy will look at the training investment and make sure that the money is used to develop and maintain a suitably skilled workforce.

Perhaps the key to successful investment in training is the creation of a learning organization where every individual recognizes their own potential for growth and performance improvement.

Key points

- Training has a significant beneficial impact on profits.
- Investment in people via training should produce an effective and measurable payback.
- Investment appraisal techniques should be used to show the returns from training.

- To quantify benefits it is necessary to know how the improvement in individual performance affects profit.
- Every employee has an impact on profit.
- Carrying out a performance audit is the essential first step in a training audit which will identify:
  —where training can produce the greatest benefits;
  —where present training activities are ineffective;
  —the extent and use of the training budget;
  —how the training budget can be re-directed to greater effect; and
  —where the training budget can be increased to reap benefits from unharvested fields.
- The full life-cycle cost of training should be appraised.
- Every employee should have a personal 'objectives and impact' statement.

PART THREE

New training skills and techniques

7 New training techniques

In the rapidly changing future that awaits everyone a great deal of learning will take place with, around, or directly involving computers. This tends to have a dehumanizing effect on the learning process, and it is perfectly possible for systems-training programmes to treat the learners as extensions of the computer system. It is, in my mind, essential that the human aspect of learning is not forgotten, and that techniques are used that fully recognize that people, and not computers, are the primary concern.

In the title of this chapter I have used the word 'new'. Some readers may feel that the techniques I am describing as new are simply a re-defined way of looking at techniques that have been around for some time. My justification for using the word new is that I believe the techniques I am describing are a new way of looking at training. In developing 'new' perspectives everyone stands on the shoulders of those who have gone before, and if this is evident in this chapter then I am delighted.

The 'new' techniques that I am going to describe are:

- Positive learning
- Dynamic learning
- Enquiry learning
- Personal Motivation Coaching

All of these techniques are learning centred, and are used to put learners in touch with their inherent learning skills. They are all ways of trying to recapture the learning power everyone had as new-born human beings. They are I believe applicable to all forms of training whether or not technology is used to help deliver the training to the learner.

Positive learning

During the past fifteen years I have experienced a large amount of negative learning, and I have played my part in using the negative learning approach in my work. I have now come to realize that it is not nearly as effective as it is believed to be. There have been a whole string of films and videos made, many of them verging on television comedy, which show the problems when things go wrong as a way of explaining the right way to do things. Learners enjoy the humour, and pick up learning points on the basis of 'I must remember not to do that', but when they are asked 'what should you do?' it is much more difficult to get a sensible answer.

Positive learning is concerned with concentrating at all times on the correct way to do things. This applies to all the materials used in the training, as well as to the training approach used. To succeed in producing positive learning programmes five main things have to be considered:

- Negative words are to be avoided. The words NO, NOT, DON'T, CANNOT, CAN'T, etc. are taboo.
- Examples and demonstrations are always what *should be known and done.*
- Exercises and case studies should always seek to establish what *should be done,* rather than what has gone wrong.
- When errors and mistakes occur, as they will, the response is *'this is how you should do it',* rather than 'this is what you did wrong'.
- Assessments of performance should be reported on the basis of the *'success rate'* rather than the 'error rate'.

Positive learning means that people learn from their mistakes, but not by concentrating on what went wrong, this only reinforces bad practice. When people perform inappropriately, i.e. they fail or do something wrong, the positive approach is to concentrate on what should have been done to improve performance. In this way the learning is positive and directed to doing things in the best way.

Negative words

People have become so used to using negative words in the way they express themselves, both orally and in writing, that they find it very hard to eliminate them from their vocabulary. However, once one starts to think about positive writing and speaking, it becomes easier and easier to avoid using negative words. I believe that avoiding negative words improves the quality of the message. Here are a couple of examples:

Negative If your potential customer is speaking you should not interrupt, and you should not ignore clear buying signals or you won't get an order.

Positive When your potential customer is speaking you should listen carefully especially to pick up buying signals, which will enable you to ask for an order.

Negative Whatever you do don't use the red fire extinguisher when the fire involves electrical equipment. The extinguisher will not put the fire out, and it could harm you.

Positive Electrical fires must be tackled with the blue fire extinguisher. The red extinguisher is for fires involving wood, paper, and fabric. If you use the red extinguisher on electrical fires you could be harmed.

Examples and demonstrations

It may be fun to show things going wrong; it may serve as a way of grabbing people's attention. It is quite understandable that trainers should use examples of things going wrong as an entertaining form of training.

But what is entertaining is not necessarily the best way to get the message to the learner. A good example of how to do something properly, followed by a discussion that seeks to elicit from the learner what was being done to produce the successful results, is a powerful learning tool. It may not be as humorous as seeing somebody do it wrong, but it makes the learner think about what is being learned in a positive way.

Why is it that people are entertained by seeing others slip on banana skins? Why is there enjoyment in someone else's discomfort? And what is learned from such examples? People learn that if they make mistakes, or get into a difficult situation they are going to be laughed at and ridiculed, which will hardly encourage them to risk making mistakes.

Errors and mistakes

I have always wondered why supervisors and managers seem to spend a lot of their time picking up people's mistakes, and then reprimanding them. How much better to pick up success and praise people, and when mistakes do occur help people to learn how to do it right. However well people are trained they will make mistakes. I am not suggesting that this is ignored, but that it is not made a big issue, and that the concentration is on 'doing things right'.

During a skiing lesson I was having a particular problem that I just couldn't master. The instructor showed me several times what I was doing wrong, and I just got worse. I finally pleaded with him to show me exactly how I SHOULD do it, and to tell me when I got it RIGHT, not when I got it wrong. I soon solved the problem, and started to ski much better. I am currently having the same problem with my golf instructor.

Assessments

People are more encouraged, and learn more when they are assessed on the basis of what they have done right. This means setting performance targets that are positive, i.e.. that state what the learner's success rate is. This is the easiest part of positive learning to implement.

It has been common practice in the education system of most countries to mark on the basis of what has been got right, so the approach to measuring and reporting success is already well established. It is important to add to the 'success rating' advice that will help learners to take a very positive approach to improving their performance. This advice should always concentrate on how performance can be improved by some positive action, 'If you do this then this will improve', rather than 'If you stop doing this'. People find it very hard to stop doing something that has become a bad habit. Telling them not to do something is never as good as suggesting what they should do, in fact it often reinforces the very problem that they are trying to overcome.

Dynamic learning

This is a technique which I know is the best way for me to learn. My inherent learning skills thrive when I am presented with an exciting, challenging learning experience which is constantly changing. That is, an experience which hardly stands still long enough for me to realize what is going on. It is the constantly changing nature of the experience which gives rise to the name 'dynamic'.

A dynamic learning experience demands the complete involvement and commitment of learners to the process. It also calls for learners to take full and total responsibility for their own learning. The role of the trainer is to facilitate the experience.

Creating dynamic learning experiences calls for ingenuity and imagination. It also calls for a very carefully prepared and flexible training programme. There are five elements to dynamic learning:

- The dynamic structure
- Dynamic intervention
- Dynamic reporting
- Dynamic assessment
- Dynamic feedback

The dynamic structure

The dynamic structure requires three things to be decided, planned, and carefully prepared. These are: what is going to happen; when it is going to happen; and how it is going to happen. The learners do not of course know what the structure is. Discovery is a major learning factor in dynamic learning.

Before this structure can be created the analysis of the key learning points, which are to be built into the programme, has to be completed. Within the structure created there are three separate parts: first is a definition of the experience; second is the statement of 'learning targets'; and third is a description of the process. This is the information that is given to the learners at the beginning of the experience.

Dynamic intervention

Once the experience starts the learners are given little time to appreciate what is happening. Within a few minutes additional information is provided that could immediately change the perspective of the experience, or have no effect at all. This type of intervention continues at random times, or seemingly random times, throughout the experience. It is usual to run such experiences in small groups, and it is probable that the interventions for each group might be different in content and/or timing. It is possible to build experiences where the groups have to interrelate. Apart from the interventions the learners are left to their own devices in working through the experience. Even things like meals can be left to their own efforts.

Dynamic reporting

Some experiences may run for a single phase with reports at the end of the phase; alternatively, and preferably, reporting may be in stages at the end of which each group reports back either individually or all together. The stage may have a fixed deadline, or may be whenever a particular group is ready. The learners have to report without any guidance on what to report, or what the consequent interventions might be. As can be seen the experience is truly dynamic and creates a situation where learners are forced to abandon the learning approaches they have been conditioned to use, and rely entirely on their inherent learning skills.

Dynamic assessment

In a dynamic learning experience, assessment should be continuous and positive, unless it is decided to generate a particular learning activity by deliberately using negative motivation. Learners need to know how well they are doing during the experience. This information is both encouraging and stimulating and maintains the level of commitment. So assessment is made as each group reaches a certain stage in the learning experience. The assessment should relate to the learning that is taking place, rather than the progress of the experience, but it should relate to the experience.

People taking part in learning experiences very quickly get lost in the experience itself, and frequently fail to recognize that learning is taking place. It is important to use the assessment to reinforce the knowledge and acceptance of the learning that is happening.

Dynamic feedback Dynamic feedback is the continuous process of maintaining the motivation and commitment of individuals taking part in the learning experience. This is different from the assessment of how well the experience is going. Feedback involves information about what is happening, and how people may be feeling. It will include dealing with questions and problems that arise, and dealing with personal relationships in the groups. It is good learning experience to let people sort out their own difficulties, but it will be necessary to encourage them to do that, and to let them know that what is happening is OK.

Dynamic learning is a difficult technique for the trainer to use. It calls for a high degree of planning and preparation. Trainers need considerable facilitation skills, and a learning-centred approach to training, to enable them to facilitate dynamic learning successfully.

Enquiry learning

I started using enquiry learning by accident.

I was asked to give a talk to a group of senior managers on the subject of communication skills. I had prepared my talk, and a set of visual aids on both overhead projector foils and 35mm slides. I travelled by air to where I was to give my talk. I waited patiently at the airport carousel for the suitcase, which contained my clothes and materials, to arrive. Needless to say it didn't. I was faced with giving my talk the next day with none of my carefully prepared material. I naturally hoped the suitcase would arrive in time and in fact it caught up with me two days later.

The morning of the talk arrived and I was introduced to the managers. My opening words were, 'Good morning ladies and gentlemen, I have been asked to talk to you about communications, now this is a big subject and could cover all kinds of things, but I would like to start by asking you to communicate your needs to me by asking me the questions uppermost in your minds about communications'.

After a short silence a question came, then another, and another, and so on. Sometimes I asked questions back, and a highly animated, participative learning experience took place. Much of the material we dealt with was in my original notes, but we also covered a great deal I had not even thought of.

I realized that here was an approach that, provided I had prepared extensively in advance, I could use to great effect. Since this first experience of enquiry learning I have used the approach often, and I have come to recognize that it is so successful because it is based on one of the inherent learning skills everyone has, and one which is a key learning motivator—curiosity.

In order to use enquiry learning with confidence it is beneficial to prepare the material that it is thought will be needed, preferably in separate modules dealing with the main questions that are anticipated. In addition I also like to prepare a series of questions I can ask the learners, if their questions dry up. I have found that this rarely happens, and I have never had a situation where people are bored, restless, or falling asleep, nor has anyone walked out on an enquiry learning experience. It is not a difficult approach, but it takes confidence and a good facilitation style to make it work well.

Personal motivation coaching

The word motivation is widely used, but not often fully understood. It is central to the approach I am going to describe, so it is important to start with a clear definition.

The *Oxford English Dictionary* (OED) gives the following definition: 'The act of moving or inducing a person to act in a certain way; a desire, fear, reason, etc., which influences a person's volition.'

The *Universal Dictionary:* 'The mental process, function, or instinct that produces and sustains incentive or drive in human and animal behaviour.'

Both of these definitions imply that motivation is some kind of force or power that determines the way people act. Neither definition attempts to state where this force or power comes from. I believe, and my approach is based on this belief, that motivation is the inner fire that burns within everyone. It is there all the time, and is fuelled by all the past experience and conditioning that people have had. It is stimulated both by people's thoughts and by external events that occur in their personal environment.

The definition of motivation that I believe is most appropriate is,

'The inner force that makes each person pursue courses of action, both positive and negative, which lead to the satisfaction of some personal desire.'

Personal motivation coaching is a continuous process where this inner force is examined, and the impact that external stimuli have on motivation is assessed. This allows individuals to begin to understand their inner life force, and to begin to take steps to harness it for personal growth and achievement. I believe it is vital for personnel and training managers to recognize the power of harnessing this inner drive that exists in everyone.

This process can only be carried out by people themselves, but they can be helped by counselling from others who understand the process. This counselling is a form of coaching which seeks to guide and encourage individuals as they progress.

Gradually people begin to be able to understand and control their inner life force, and to use it to reach levels of achievement they had never dreamed possible. They begin to discover what they really want from life, and learn how to get it.

Personal motivation coaching is not difficult to describe, or to understand. It is possible for people to follow the process without any counselling. It does, however, require a continuous commitment, and counselling is a great help in maintaining resolve.

The four steps to growth

To aspire to their personal fulfilment everyone needs to have a clear grasp of the things that will help and hinder them. In addition they need to understand their boundaries, both those they set themselves, and the ones imposed upon them by other people. Finally they have to know how to find the space to breathe and grow.

Building blocks

No one can go back and change the past. Whatever has happened to make people who they are, has already taken place. Many people don't welcome the prospect of making a careful assessment of themselves, but they need to do so before they can move on.

They need to discover their real strengths, which includes their personality strengths as well as their skills. These will then become the building blocks on which they can create the foundation of their future growth.

Barriers

There are a great many things that people allow to get in their way. Most of these barriers are self-created. They are the result of many years of conditioning about what people can and can't do. If someone tells people frequently that they are useless, they come to believe it, just as they believe it if someone tells them how good they are. But isn't it interesting that people are always more ready to believe the bad things about themselves than the good things. People now have to identify all the barriers to their growth, and then start to tear them down systematically.

Boundaries

Just as people have been conditioned to accept barriers to their personal achievement, so they have been conditioned to accept boundaries to their growth. Statements such as,
'Don't forget your working-class background.'
'You're not intelligent enough to get a degree.'
'No one in our family has ever done manual work.'
all conspire to establish boundaries to their lives.

People need to establish the boundaries that surround them now; then they can start to stretch them further and further until finally they have no limits to their growth.

Breathing space

For personal motivation coaching to be effective it has to become a regular part of everyday activities. From time to time people have to review the four key steps. Many things will change and, it is hoped, will keep changing for the better. It is crucial that people make space for themselves to think, to learn, and to grow.

The space can be alone, or with someone else; indoors, or outdoors; or wherever they feel comfortable and relaxed. Once they have created the space, when and where they want it, they should use it to assess and re-assess where they are, and where they want to be. When they are satisfied that they have breathed in sufficient freshness, they can return.

The three tasks

Personal motivation coaching is a gentle process: people involved in it should be happy and relaxed. If it becomes a chore, something they feel they have to do, then they will get little if any benefit. People should be able to have fun, and it often helps to share thoughts and feelings with others who are using personal motivation coaching. This is particularly so with the three tasks, which are: the potential profile, the aspiration statement, and personal affirmations.

Potential profile

The potential profile is a statement of individual strengths under four main headings:

- superb at
- brilliant at
- my wonderful features
- reasons I am totally lovable

At first sight many people will recoil with the feeling that they couldn't possibly write down such things about themselves. This is perfectly understandable. Until now they have only been allowed to state what they are no good at, to denigrate themselves, and to reinforce all the conditioning they have received. The older they are the worse it it. Now is the chance to break this destructive pattern and to recognize the enormous potential that lies within everyone. People can't do this unless they come to know and believe in themselves. The potential profile is their first step.

Aspiration statement

Once they have completed their potential profile they will be in a good position to think about where they want to be in the future. The first step is to imagine, assuming everything is possible, where they want to be in three years time.

They can now look at their potential profile and see how everything they aspire to is possible. You see people do already know what they can achieve, they just keep it hidden because it frightens them.

Personal affirmations

Because people have been so thoroughly conditioned in the past, mostly to believe lies about themselves, they now have to start conditioning themselves to believe the truth. Affirmations are statements that people can regularly make to themselves until the truth is firmly embedded in their subconscious. Here are a few of my affirmations:
'I am a talented and creative writer.'
'I have the power to love unconditionally.'
'I have everything I need to make me happy.'
'I can build beautiful relationships, now.'

Many people are uneasy with the idea of affirmations, some even think the idea silly and ineffective. Unfortunately the effect of negative affirmations is only too apparent in everyone's life. People only have to tell themselves that they can't do something, or that they will do it wrong, and what happens? Positive affirmations are only the reverse of this, and are just as effective.

These three tasks are carried out continuously. People's potential profiles are extended, their aspiration statements amended as they achieve more and more, and their affirmations changed, as they discard those they no longer need and add new ones.

Coaching themselves

Is it possible for people to coach themselves? Many people identify coaching with being shown what to do by someone who has superior knowledge, and who can inspire them. In personal motivation coaching people are their own coaches. The key elements of coaching are, observation, reinforcement, encouragement, and guidance.

It is perfectly possible, during their breathing space, for people to observe what has been happening to them and how they have responded. By using their affirmations they can reinforce their positive aspects. Their successes will provide encouragement to continue, as will reference to their aspiration statement. Guidance will come from continuous reappraisal of their potential profile.

Using personal motivation coaching releases enormous reserves of energy, and directs people to the most positive aspects of their lives. No one else can motivate them. All their motivation comes from their inner selves. External events, particularly their own success, stimulate them to use their inner force in the way they feel best. But in the end their success and happiness are in their own hands or, should I say, minds.

Key points

- Positive learning is concerned with concentrating at all times on the correct way to do things.
- People learn from their mistakes by discovering positive ways to do things well.
- Inherent learning skills thrive when presented with exciting and challenging experiences which are constantly changing.
- People absorb information when it is given in response to enquiries they make.
- Curiosity is a powerful inherent learning skill.
- Motivation is:
  'The inner force that makes each person pursue courses of action, both positive and negative, that lead to the satisfaction of some personal desire.'
- Counselling is a form of coaching that seeks to guide and encourage people in their progress.
- In personal motivation coaching there are four steps to personal growth:
  —building blocks (personal strengths);
  —barriers (self-created);
  —boundaries (conditioned limitations); and
  —breathing space (time and space to grow).
- There are three tasks;
  —create a potential profile;
  —write an aspiration statement; and
  —produce and use personal affirmations.
- Self-coaching is a process of self-observation, self-reinforcement, self-encouragement, and self-guidance.
- People only learn what they want to learn;
  people only succeed when they want to;
  people only grow if they nourish themselves;
  people know themselves better than anyone else;
  people are the source of their own energy and power, and they are the only ones who can motivate themselves

8 The new training skills

Trainers gather their skills from a wide arena. Some come from formal exposure to training on 'train the trainer' workshops, some come from attending courses and 'watching' other people train, and some, perhaps the largest slice, come from the experience of actually training others. These skills can be described in a variety of ways. In this chapter I am going to look at the 'new' skills trainers need in order to cope with the training demands of a high tech future.

Once again it is possible that some trainers reading this book will argue with my decision to call the skills described in this chapter as 'new'. They will feel that many of these skills have always been needed by good trainers, and this is probably true. However, in my experience of trainer training programmes few if any of these skills are included on the agenda. It is for this reason that I describe these skills as 'new'.

The skills I am going to describe are in most cases in addition to traditional skills, but some will replace existing skills. I have decided to separate the 'new' skills into seven categories, which are:

- Technical skills
- Analytical skills
- Design skills
- Communication skills
- Psychology skills
- Facilitation skills
- Counselling skills

Technical skills

The trainer has always needed to keep up to date with technical advances. This has meant trainers being able to use video equipment and closed circuit television; all kinds of visual display equipment; sound control equipment and multi-translation facilities.

Even if trainers do not become fully-trained technicians, they still need to have a good understanding of the technical equipment they use. Now the trainer faces the need to come to terms with a new range of technical skills. Some trainers have already started along this road, but many haven't.

The new technical skills are:

- Computer use, including programming
- Communication networks

- Computer-based graphics
- Desktop publishing

Computer use

Trainers will have to be able to use the computer for both personal and training purposes. This will include being able to operate a word processing facility, use spread sheets, use planning tools, understand computer based training (CBT) authoring software, and even write programs where the training software requires it. In addition trainers of the future will have to be able to converse with computer and systems specialists to make sure they get what they want from the computer. As more and more training becomes 'technology' training, trainers will have to develop an understanding of the technology. This will then help them to create 'technology-based' training.

Communication networks

I once had a discussion with a systems engineer about the possibility of keeping the library of training modules on the central mainframe, and downloading them to personal computers (PCs) as and when the PC user wanted to call for them. The systems engineer spent about twenty minutes explaining why this was not technically possible at the present time. I believed it was possible, but I couldn't find any technical evidence to support my argument. A few weeks later, using an excellent piece of software called 'Automator mi', I was able to demonstrate to the systems engineer how it could be done.

Technical information of the functioning of networks and data transfer will enable trainers to make the best use of computers for training, including such things as videotex. This is a much misunderstood and underutilized technology. Essentially it is a very simple way of presenting pages of text and graphics on television monitors. These are relatively inexpensive. With a little imagination programmed learning can be built and delivered to widely scattered audiences at a low cost.

Computer-based graphics

The days of paper-based graphic artwork are over for those who can afford the computer-based alternative. The power of the graphics computer has to be seen to be believed. Not only is the range, both in design and colour almost unlimited, but all kinds of figures, symbols, pictures, etc. can be held on file. They can be called when needed, and reduced or enlarged to fit a particular need. Once the design is agreed it can be printed, filmed onto overhead projector (OHP) foils, or 35mm slides. The cost is now such that it is becoming cheaper than the alternative paper-based method.

Desktop publishing

Written training materials can now incorporate different styles and sizes of typeface, diagrams, pictures, and so on. The quality of reproduction is so good that there is no longer any excuse for poor training materials. The skill of being able to use, or specify exactly what is required from, desktop publishing is an essential one.

These technical skills may not appeal to some trainers. They might believe that using technology gets in the way of using intuition and being creative. But this need not be the case. In fact it is quite possible that a good understanding of technical issues could help trainers to be even more creative than in the past.

Analytical skills

In Chapter 11 I look at the use of the learning-centred design methodology as a key analytical tool for trainers. To use the methodology, trainers will have to have the necessary analytical skills. These can be examined under four headings:

- questioning
- interpretation
- logic
- synthesis

Questioning

Asking questions, particularly the right ones, is an acquired analytical skill. The difference between 'open' and 'closed' questions has to be understood, and the way that questions can be asked has to be known and practised. The reward of a good questioning skill is that you gather the information needed, which is accurate and complete. This in turn considerably improves the quality of the analysis of training and learning needs, and results in a better training solution.

Interpretation

Once the answers to the questions have been gathered they have to be interpreted within the context of the analysis taking place. This calls for the ability to be able to think clearly what the implications of the answers are, and to interpret these in terms of training and learning needs. Interpretation is the process of recognizing the significance and meaning of the information to hand, and this is very important in the development of good training.

Logic

Logic is the process of reasoning that seeks to clarify the relationship of a set of objects, individuals, principles, or events. It is particularly important in structured task analysis, and in deciding the best sequence in which to cover learning needs. Applying logic does not mean ignoring intuition, in fact quite the contrary. When the basic approach is logical there is much more scope for using intuition, and being creative within the logical framework.

Synthesis

The process of synthesis is ideally explained by this extract from the little red book of Mao Tse Tung.

> Go to the practical people and learn from them: then synthesize their experience into principles and theories: and then return to the practical people and call upon them to put these principles and methods into practice so as to solve their problems and achieve freedom and happiness.

Design skills

Design of training programmes is part of the learning-centred design methodology, but following the methodology does require basic design skills. These involve being able to review the outcome of the analysis stage, and to develop an imaginative approach to building the training programme to meet the training and learning needs.

Design skills fall into three sections:

- perception
- imagination
- execution

Perception Perception is the ability to gain an understanding and insight into what the training programme is trying to achieve, and to use intuition in the formulation of an effective approach. To be able to 'see' where people are going and how they are going to get there is crucial to designing and building a successful training programme.

Imagination To be able to mentally 'picture' the training programme, and to develop innovative approaches to how learning points can be handled, is the art of imagination. I call it an art because it is difficult to consider imagination as being in any way scientific. People who have a good vivid imagination have an advantage, but it is possible to learn how to develop imaginative thinking. The reason some people think they lack an imagination is because they have never had the opportunity to give free reign to their inherent skill to think imaginatively.

Execution To transfer a design into a finished workable training programme, whether this be computer-based, dynamic learning, enquiry learning, or traditional paper-based training, it is a distinct advantage for trainers to have the skill to carry out the detailed work themselves. It can of course be delegated, but trainers need to be able to manage the production process effectively. Part of the design skill is being able to specify and present ideas to others so that they can readily understand what is wanted, and how it needs to be done. This clarity in explanation is an essential feature of good design, and could include using such techniques as flowcharting and decision trees.

Communication skills

Using the written and spoken word effectively is a basic requirement for all trainers. In the world of high tech it is of no less importance than it has ever been. The ways to communicate are changing all the time, with new facilities being added to the existing ones. Such facilities as video conferencing, private viewdata, portable telephones, optical cable, and satellites are all bringing increasing pressure on good communication.

Trainers of the future will have to know how to make the best use of all communication media, as well as being excellent communicators. As techniques such as distance learning harness the power of modern communications it becomes necessary to design and build training programmes that rely on these new media for their success. This means being able to understand and use the media to the best effect possible. Never forget that, though the method of delivery is important, what really matters is the message itself. This has to be clear, simple and brief, no matter which medium is used.

Psychology skills

It has always been important for trainers to have a sound grasp of psychology, but in the high tech age it takes on a different perspective. The interface between people and machines now becomes an important issue. In the past it was only the interface between people and people that had to be thought about. There are three aspects of psychology that I will look at in this chapter. These are:

- psychology of learning

- psychology of risking
- psychology of human–machine interface

Psychology of learning

There are many views and opinions regarding the psychology of learning, particularly with reference to the differences between the learning skills of people at different ages. I want to suggest that everyone is born with an immense range of powers which are displayed by new-born infants, and which are used during the first few years of life. People are born with the ability to communicate their needs in a very direct and effective way. If any needs are not met they are able to discharge their feelings in a totally natural and unhampered form. Crying and screaming, laughing and loving are all inherent powers that the new-born child does not have to learn.

The new-born child also has the power to walk, talk, read, write, paint and so on. It can't immediately do these things because it hasn't yet discovered that it has the power to do them. What happens is that the new-born child starts on a wonderful journey of discovery.

Using all its inherent powers the child listens, watches, touches, tastes, and feels everything going on around it. Nothing seems beyond its innate curiosity. It absorbs its immediate environment like a sponge. In a few months the power of the child's inherent learning skills is apparent. It learns quickly what to do to get attention. This does of course vary from family to family, but the child learns exactly what to do in its own particular environment. It learns to walk and talk, with or without encouragement. Those that do receive encouragement seem to learn earlier than those that don't. With the ability to talk comes the never-ending stream of questions. Questions that are asked repeatedly until the young child receives an answer that fits its current understanding. And so the process continues, with the child's inherent learning needs being constantly fed by its environment.

When the child reaches a certain age (different in different societies) it is transferred from its home environment into the new learning environment of school. Here the child is expected to respond in certain ways to the needs that others, particularly its teachers and parents, have for it to learn. Slowly but surely the inherent learning skills are shut off. Curiosity, involvement, and exploration are actively discouraged, unless they relate to the subject being 'taught'. If the child takes an interest in something in the environment it is seen as a distraction, and the child is directed back to what the teacher thinks should be learned.

There are, of course, schools where the inherent learning skills are allowed to flourish and grow, but these are seen as unusual attempts to allow children to learn through playing and being, and are ridiculed by many traditional educationalists.

In the traditional school system the child's inherent skills and desire to explore, experiment, and discover are gradually shut down. The child who does persist in this approach is chastised, marked down, and ridiculed. People shut down their inherent learning skills and replace them with enforced learning of subjects, for the most part of no apparent relevance or interest to them.

What is happening is a slow process of conditioning to the acceptance that what people learn is what they are fed by their teachers. There is little place for the free run of their inherent learning skills. The need people have to explore what interests them is replaced with a need to 'take in' what they are taught. It becomes more a process of memory development than learning. Teachers become providers of knowledge, instead of being guides to learning.

This process continues right into adulthood. Most adults have had thirteen-plus years of active conditioning in being taught, rather than learning. The inherent learning skills of adults have been almost totally suppressed. However, these skills have not been lost: they are still there.

Rediscovering inherent learning skills is an important task for everybody, especially trainers. People's inherent learning skills enable them to use all their senses to discover from experience what they feel they need to learn. Once people are interested they consciously, or unconsciously, draw on their inherent learning skills. Once their curiosity is stimulated they want to ask questions, to explore, to experiment and to discover the knowledge that awaits their enquiry. Some adults discover this power to learn without realizing that they have simply rediscovered what they already had as young children. There are psychologists who believe that adult learning is different to child learning, but strip away the adult's conditioning to learn in an inappropriate way, and we return unfailingly to the person's inherent learning skills.

All that I discuss in this book is based on the release of inherent learning skills. I am attempting to help trainers to see that the minds of children and adults are waiting eagerly to be given the opportunity to learn in a way that enables them to use the learning skills they were born with. This ability to help people rediscover the power of their inherent learning skills is a vital one for all trainers to develop.

Psychology of risking

Doing anything new for the first time means taking a risk. Some people go right ahead and have a go, others stand back and hesitate. Some people seem to enjoy taking risks, others hate the idea of taking any kind of risk. Why?

Perhaps it depends on what happens when people first take a risk in their lives. Did they succeed, or fail? If they failed what happened? Were they scolded, chastised, ridiculed, or were they told it was OK to fail, and encouraged to try again? Were they protected from taking risks? Were they offered love only if they were 'a good boy or girl'? Were they asked not to do it again because 'it upsets mummy'?

The response they received as children, and kept on receiving, is what has conditioned their adult response to risking. For people to whom failing is 'bad', taking a risk is an unnecessary way to possibly fail. So they don't succeed, because success means taking risks. For those people for whom 'to try' is more important than the outcome, whatever it is, there is no threat. For such people failure is simply a stepping-stone to success.

Learning opportunities should always be a process of taking risks. Traditional training where people sit at a lecture and are fed information involves no risk taking: it is safe. There is no pressure to learn and nothing at risk, but little real learning takes place. Learning-centred learning opportunities make it necessary for everyone involved, including the facilitator, to take risks.

Unless trainers take risks themselves, they will learn very little. Unless they learn from the experience of helping others to learn, they cannot grow and develop as good facilitators. Learning facilitation is an art that demands a range of skills often lacking in 'conventional' trainers.

Human–machine interface

Trainers working in a world of high tech will need to acquire the skills appropriate to make the human–machine interface effective. These skills include an understanding of how people react to working with the machine: the kinds of messages and responses; the layout of screens. People want to work with machines in a conversational way, but not to be patronized.

In the vast majority of systems, the machine-to-user response is equivalent to the parent–child relationship. The machine is demanding, sets rules, stops mistakes, reports errors, and rejects input. The messages the user receives are often couched in 'parental' language, 'you cannot do that, 'you must not do that'. This level of interface is unsatisfactory and causes impatience, frustration and annoyance.

What is needed is a human–machine interface that is much more the adult–adult relationship of two equals. The machine messages must be more reasoning than demanding, and use positive language, e.g. 'the data you have entered seems inappropriate, could you check and re-enter'. There may well be more words than in the standard cryptic demanding messages, but the effect is far superior.

It is desirable for the trainer to understand the psychology of the human–machine interface, and be able to help systems designers to produce systems with effective human interfaces.

Facilitation skills

Facilitation is the process of making things happen, of making things easy, and moving things, events and people forward. The facilitation of learning requires a range of skills in five categories. These are:

- preparing learning opportunities
- stimulating learning-desire
- guiding the learning process
- maintaining learning-desire
- achieving learning targets

Preparing learning opportunities

In this section I will consider the mental process of preparing to facilitate a learning opportunity. The first consideration is the degree of freedom that the learners are to be given to decide how they want to learn. If they are given complete freedom, then the facilitation task is one of helping them to follow whichever path they desire. This will mean that preparation is concerned more with establishing source and availability of learning resources, than with the provision of the resources. If freedom is limited within the time and physical constraints of a workshop, then it becomes necessary to think about the way that learning resources are to be made available.

This will probably include preparing several alternatives, including presentations with visual aids, written material, group dynamic learning exercises, discussion notes, and enquiry learning questions.

As learning opportunities have to be exciting, stimulating, and involve learners in taking risks, they have to be prepared with great care. Every possible event, every twist and turn along the road to the learning target has to be thought about. This is a skill that is only learned by people using their own inherent learning skills by experimenting, and exploring each time they facilitate a learning opportunity.

Stimulating learning-desire

Everyone enjoys learning. It is a thrilling and satisfying activity, at least it is when it's something that they want to learn. To stimulate learning-desire trainers have first of all to discover why the learners should want to learn what they are about to help them to learn. And then they have to present the learning opportunity to them in a way that invites their involvement, offers them a degree of choice, and clearly calls upon them to use their inherent learning skills.

Some years ago I was running a third-year undergraduate course in managerial economics. One section of the course dealt with economic issues of takeovers and mergers. Managerial economics is a dry subject at the best of times, and the topic I had to deal with was only one step better than monetary policy. I decided to approach the subject by asking the students if they would like to choose how to learn about takeovers and mergers. I gave them three options to choose from: lectures; deciding what they wanted to know and asking me questions (enquiry learning); or to stage a simulated takeover battle (dynamic learning). They chose the takeover battle, and for four weeks we all enjoyed a most stimulating and exciting time. Many students, for whom this was the first experience of dynamic learning, told me that learning would never be the same again.

Guiding the learning process

Imagine this to be a similar task to that of a mountain guide employed by a group of tourists to help them climb a mountain. What do the group expect of their guide? I would think that they would expect the guide to fine a route that they can manage; to check that they are properly equipped for the journey; to provide assistance if they get stuck; to help them choose the best path; to protect them and keep them safe; to give them first aid if they need it; to watch the weather for changes; and to show them everything of interest on the route. In addition they would certainly expect the guide to know the terrain, and to be properly equipped.

Guiding people through a learning experience is almost exactly the same process. As guides trainers have to respond to the needs of the learners, rather than have the learners respond to the trainers' needs. When acting as a guide it is possible to work from three positions; out in front with the group following; at the back with the group wandering in front; or in the middle as a part of the group. I personally like to guide as a part of the group, but the other ways can work quite well, depending upon the trainer's style and skill.

Guiding people through the learning opportunity also means being able to intervene gently, guiding rather than directing, nudging rather than pushing, encouraging rather than criticizing. Intervention skills are perhaps the most important and difficult of facilitation skills. Knowing when and how to intervene comes with experience, but the good facilitator concentrates more on not intervening, leaving the group to find their own solutions. The signals for intervention are when the group are clearly stuck; when side arguments develop; when someone is distressed, but not to stop the distress: rather to help the person deal with it; when the group request help; and when the group have strayed too far from the path. At all times the intervention should be as gentle as possible.

Maintaining learning-desire

There are times during a learning opportunity when learners find their learning-desire fading. Just like the tourists climbing the mountain they may wish they had never started. What does the guide do to maintain the desire to continue? The first thing is to be aware of the condition of the group. If they are tired, then a rest or a diversion may be called for. It may be necessary to change direction, and by asking the group what they want to do it is likely that they will want a change. Just by making a choice the learners will be restimulated and feel in control of what is happening.

Maintaining learning-desire is a combination of feeding the learning demands, and yet generating sufficient curiosity to maintain interest. However, if curiosity is left unsatisfied for too long the effect is a negative one, and learners may switch off.

Achieving learning targets

Whose targets are trainers trying to achieve? Which is the most important, what trainers want the learners to learn, what trainers want to learn, or what the learners want to learn?

The learning journey may start with all three of these targets quite clear in people's minds, but as professional guides trainers have to consider their customer's target to be the most important. Trainers must make sure that at the beginning of the journey they check and agree the learning targets with the learners. This will help the trainers to guide the learners to their target, and it will help the learners to recognize what their target is. It is possible that during the journey the targets will be adjusted, but as long as this is done by agreement then it is OK.

At the end of the journey it is always good to check whether everyone involved feels that the targets have been achieved, and if not, is it clear why not?

Counselling skills

The vast majority of people do not get the opportunity to counsel others, or to be counselled. Everyone needs and craves for someone to pay attention, to really listen to them, and where appropriate to allow them to discharge their feelings. This is what counselling is all about. It is not about advising, or rescuing people from their problems. The process of talking about some problem or difficulty, or how people feel, is a healing process. After a counselling session where individuals have been able to speak their minds to attentive, loving people, they feel much better.

Trainers have an ideal opportunity to counsel, and be counselled by their colleagues, and by learners. If trainers want to counsel then they have to develop several skills. These are:

- listening
- encouraging
- questioning
- contradicting

Listening

The majority of people have the natural ability to hear, but this does not necessarily mean they have developed the skill of listening. Listening is the act of concentrating on particular sounds that are heard. It takes considerable effort to listen attentively, cutting out all the extraneous noise in the environment. People cannot listen and think about something else at the same time. They cannot listen and speak at the same time. It is hard to listen without paying attention to the speaker. In counselling, paying interested attention and listening to every word is crucial to a successful outcome.

The very best counsellors listen a lot, and talk little. The key to successful counselling is giving the people being counselled the time, space and attention to get in touch with their feelings. This is done by listening, not talking.

Encouraging

During a counselling session the counsellor should give as much encouragement as possible when the person being counselled is hesitating or holding back. This encouragement might simply be a few words, or a smile, or a squeeze of the hand. Some signal that says 'I am here, and I want to listen to you.'

Encouragement does not need to be extravagant or dramatic—just a simple indication of support. During counselling people being counselled may laugh, cry, shake, yawn, scream, or tremble, all of which indicate that they are discharging old hurts, and are in the process of healing. These responses should be encouraged: people should be made to feel that it is OK to discharge in this way. The worst thing to do would be to cut off the discharge with comments such as 'don't cry—it will be all right'.

Questioning

It is perfectly natural for the counsellor to want to ask questions, but these questions should not be to satisfy the counsellor's own curiosity. They should be to help the people being counselled to say what they want. Counsellors have to resist the temptation to ask for details about events and situations, unless it is to clarify and understand the information, and to help to facilitate what the person being counselled wants to talk about.

A good question to ask might be, 'why do you think you feel this way about . . .?', or 'would you like to say something about . . .?'. These are questions which let people know that the counsellor is interested, and paying attention to what they are saying, without prying.

Contradicting

One of the keys to good counselling, is being able to contradict a person's distress. When people say they are no good, it is no benefit to them to sit there nodding. This just confirms their bad feelings. It is much better to say something like, 'I disagree, I think you are very important', or if the person says, 'I hate myself', the counsellor can respond with, 'well I don't hate you'.

Another form of contradiction is to get people to change direction from negative things to good things. If they are talking about what they are no good at, switch them to talk about what are they good at, by saying, 'I don't agree, you are good at many things, just tell me something you are good at'.

Contradiction makes people being counselled rethink what they are saying, makes them realize that their counsellor is not going to sit and collude with their self-doubt. This brings them to face their own feelings and to discharge any distress they may have.

Counselling is a skill that should be an attribute of good trainers. To be able to counsel well will enable good trainers really to 'help people to learn', and this is what training is all about. A humanistic approach to training, putting the learner first, and concentrating on the learning process itself, are keys to successful training.

Key points

- 'To learn is a natural pleasure not confined to philosophers, but common to all men.' (Aristotle)
- Trainers need technical skills in:
  —computer use, including programming;
  —communication networks;
  —computer based graphics; and
  —desktop publishing.
- Analytical skills are needed for:
  —questioning;
  —interpretation;
  —logic; and
  —synthesis.
- Design skills fall into three sections:
  —perception;
  —imagination; and
  —execution.
- Successful communication relies on messages that are clear, simple and brief, no matter which medium is used.
- Trainers need to be skilled in the psychology of:
  —learning;
  —risking; and
  —the human–machine interface.
- People are slowly conditioned to accept being taught, and gradually lose sight of their inherent learning skills.

- Rediscovering inherent learning skills is an important task for everyone, especially trainers.
- What is needed is a human–machine interface that is an adult–adult interaction of two equals.
- Facilitation is the process of making things happen, of making things easy, and moving things and people forward.
- Everyone needs and craves for someone to pay attention and really listen to them.
- The best counsellors listen a lot and say little.

9 The training spectrum

When experienced trainers come into contact with the learning-centred approach many of them assume that this is only applicable to personal development training, and that other forms of training have to be handled differently. I believe that the learning-centred approach applies to all forms of training and across the full range of the training spectrum.

I define the 'training spectrum' as a continuum of training approaches going from 'highly non-directive' to 'highly directive'. This can be shown on a simple chart. (Figure 9.1)

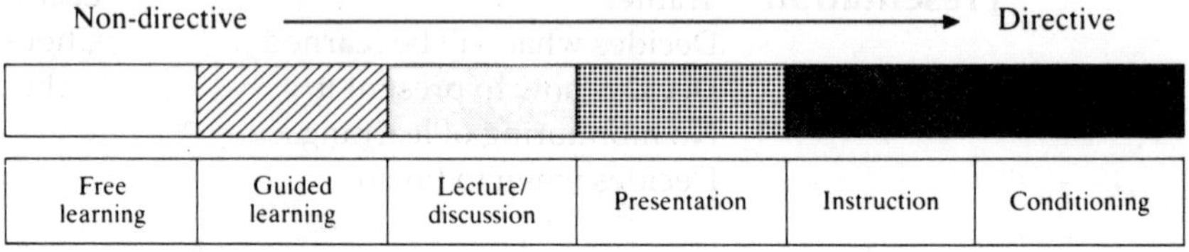

Figure 9.1 *The training spectrum*

The six stages of the spectrum are used purely as an indicator of the way in which the roles of trainer and learner change. The spectrum flows smoothly across from 'free learning' to 'conditioning'. There are no clearly defined lines to draw, and there is much overlap.

A learning-centred approach can be applied right across the spectrum. It is more difficult to see how 'instruction' or 'conditioning' can be learning centred, but if the learners have specifically asked for some instruction, or to be conditioned to cope with extremes of temperature, for example, then this is learning centred. It ceases to be learning centred when the learners have no control over the training process.

The six categories of training used in the chart are described below by taking the learner's and the trainer's perspective for each.

Free learning

Learner	Trainer
Chooses what to learn.	Provides opportunity, environment and resources
Chooses how to learn.	
Decides on resources used.	
Monitors own learning.	
Finishes when satisfied with own learning.	

Guided learning

Learner	**Trainer**
Chooses what to learn. Seeks guidance in how to learn. Uses resources provided. Seeks help in monitoring learning. Finishes when learner and trainer are satisfied.	Provides guidance on how to learn. Provides specific resources to aid learning. Helps to monitor learning. Agrees with learner when to finish.

Lecture/discussion

Learner	**Trainer**
Chooses what to listen to. No choice on how to learn. Takes resources given and questions value. Answers tests. Is advised on learning. Finishes when trainer decides.	Decides what to impart. Decides sequence and relevance. Answers questions. Sets tests. Advises on learning progress. Decides when to finish.

You will notice that for the next three the trainer comes first:

Presentation

Trainer	**Learner**
Decides what will be learned. Decides how to present it. No monitoring of learning. Decides when to finish.	Chooses what to learn from the presentation.

Instruction

Trainer	**Learner**
Decides what must be learned. Decides best way to learn. Decides resources to be given. Tests learning. Finishes when test scores OK.	No choice about what or how to learn. Must accept what is given. Must answer/pass tests. Rewarded if successful.

Conditioning

Trainer	**Learner**
Decides what is to be learned. Decides how to teach it. Decides resources given. Decides on conditioning process. Tests and repeats until conditioning OK.	No choice. Must become instinctive performer. Punished if fails.

In the training spectrum I use the terms *directive* and *non-directive* to describe the extremes of the continuum. We can see that as we become more directive the learner has less and less freedom, finally having none.

Most traditional training falls into the more directive stages while learning-centred training mostly falls into the non-directive stages. However, the learning-centred approach should not be confused with 'experiential' training which can be highly directive in the way the experience is presented, nor should it be confused with 'participative' training which often controls and directs the participation. Participation in the learning-centred approach is crucial. So here are some ideas about participation and its relevance to learning-centred training.

Participation

Many people believe that getting people to participate makes the learning more non-directive, but this depends entirely upon how the participation is handled. Here are a few examples:

Tests/examinations these are usually *highly directive* demanding answers to specific questions, with little or no choice, nearly always counter-productive to learning.

Exercises usually *directive*, in that a task is set with a preconceived outcome. People may be right or wrong.

Games frequently *directive*, with a strong element of competition which leads to the prospect and fear of failure.

Case studies if open and free these can be *non-directive*, but are often far too structured and tight, becoming *directive.*

Discussions if allowed to range freely, these are *non-directive*, but they are often led and controlled by trainer thus becoming *directive.*

Each way discussions where two or three people take turns to talk to each other and to listen paying close attention. Mostly *non-directive.*

Free groups here the group is allowed freedom to work on what they want in the way they want. Group formed by choice and common interest. Always *non-directive.*

Choice of activities individuals or groups choose what they want to do. Always *non-directive.*

Learner devised activities here individuals or groups actually choose their own learning activities. *Highly non-directive.*

Applicability of the learning-centred approach

There are many people who mistakenly relate learning-centred to personal development 'experiential' training. They do not believe that the learning-centred approach can be used for technical training. Here are three examples of how it can. They cover operating a machine, filling in a form, and talking to a customer.

OPERATING A MACHINE

Well here is the machine you are going to learn to operate. Have you any idea how it works, and how you might operate it?
A discussion now follows on operating the machine.

OK well let's see the machine working.

Did you see how it was operated?
Further discussion on how the machine was operated.

Who would like to have a try? (proper supervision and protection is of course essential)
Someone, or several people have a go (experimentation).

The next step is to demonstrate how the machine is operated. This is done slowly, relating the demonstration to questions that have already been asked.

The learners then take turns in operating the machine.

FILLING IN A FORM
Here is a blank form, let's see if you can fill it in. Make up any of the details you need.

Are there any points you would like to query, or questions you would like to ask?

What do you think the form is for?
Brief discussion on its use.

Explain its use, and ask 'is it a good design?'
Brief discussion on the design

OK here's some information see if you can fill the form in.

TALKING TO A CUSTOMER
When you are a customer in the bank how do you like to be treated?
Discussion follows.

Is this treatment important to you, and if so why?
Discussion follows.

How do you think customers should be talked to?
Discussion follows.

What problems can you envisage arising, can you list the key points about talking to customers, and making them feel good?

The three Ss

I believe that this is an important aspect of being able to apply the learning-centred approach to all forms of training across the training spectrum. The three Ss stand for *small, simple, successful.*

Small Take the learner on small steps, or short journeys that are easy to manage. They can still be challenging, but should not put the learners off. Activities should not take too long to complete. Exercises should have limited scope. When someone is given something to do which seems insurmountable, or too much to cope with, the motivation to learn is killed.

When we do things, or take risks to try things,
it is because we think we can do them.

Simple We should accept that simple things are easy to learn, and that complex things can become easy to learn if they are broken down into simple steps.

It is easy to make things difficult
but difficult to make things easy.

Successful I always try to ensure that learners can be successful at what they are learning. Tests and competitive games can be counterproductive because it is possible for learners to fail, or be unsuccessful. Though people learn from making mistakes, they also need to have the reward and satisfaction of success. Good trainers will, therefore, want to help people to be successful.

Developing good learning environments

In Chapter 15 I discuss the various environments in which people learn. Developing good learning environments, across the complete training spectrum, is more than just setting out the room in the best way. It has to do with the learning atmosphere in the room. A good learning-centred learning environment is one which:

Helps people to grow and develop through creating exciting, fun-filled learning opportunities that are free from fear, embarrassment, and judgement, and which are managed with a loving touch.

Loving T.O.U.C.H.

Trust each other to be doing everything possible to support everyone else in the group.

Openness to open our hearts and minds to the group and the opportunity to learn.

Understanding to treat everyone's comments with a kind, understanding attitude. Even when we don't agree, we should try to understand.

Confidentiality what we do or say stays here in this place and time.

Honesty to say what we mean, and to mean what we say.

Without this atmosphere the environment is not safe for people to explore, experiment, have fun, be foolish, make mistakes, break down old barriers, and be themselves. It is only when people have the freedom to be themselves that they really learn.

The training spectrum covers all forms of events created to help people to learn. As people choose whether or not they want to learn it is important to recognize that whichever form of training is used, i.e. whether it is highly directive, or highly non-directive, it has to place learning at the centre. Giving people the opportunity to choose what they learn and how they learn is not a luxury, it is a basic necessity, and whether they are offered a choice or not they will make their own decision about their learning, and place their own values on it.

Key points

- The training-centred approach applies to all forms of training and across the full range of the training spectrum.
- The training spectrum is the continuum of training from highly non-directive to highly directive.
- Training ceases to be learning centred when learners have no control over the training process.
- Keep training programmes small, simple, and successful.
- It is easy to make things difficult, but difficult to make things easy.
- Whether offered a choice or not people will choose what they learn and will place their own values on their learning.

PART FOUR

Training design

10 Learning-centred design

One of the biggest problems with many training programmes and materials is that they are based on assumptions, often unfounded, that the participants want to learn. If people aren't particularly interested, or actively don't want to learn, then they can't be forced to do so. This is the voluntary pattern of learning. It is also known that people learn involuntarily. They are carried along by the event and can't help themselves: they simply have to learn. Heightened levels of fear and enjoyment generate involuntary learning.

But is this experience really involuntary? Surely the individual makes a conscious, or unconscious decision to learn, before any learning actually takes place? Individuals can also 'switch off' their learning-desire, in almost any circumstance.

Learning to use computers is, for most people, a particularly unexciting prospect. There is often a lot of detailed information to be absorbed, and a lot of technical jargon to understand. In spite of this it is possible, even in the high technology environment, to capture and hold the attention of learners.

Successful training which captures and holds the participants' learning desire, or which creates heightened levels of emotional activity, must be centred on the learning that is taking place. It must in other words be 'learning centred'.

Learning-centred design is concerned with creating a situation where participants will be hard-pressed to avoid learning. There are three crucial stages in carrying out learning-centred design:

- defining learning needs;
- deciding how the audience's learning desire can be stimulated; and
- managing the learning process.

Defining learning needs

The development of most training programmes starts with a process of training-needs analysis. This process is concerned with deciding what the 'trainees' have to know and be able to do on completion of the training. This is a necessary step if trainers ever want to produce training that is effective. However, training needs are not the same as learning needs. Training needs are what the trainers want the trainee to be able to know and do, whereas learning needs are what the individuals want to know and do. If the difference is not clear then try asking a group of trainees what their learning needs are and compare them with a set of training needs.

How can we define learning needs?

The first step is to produce a statement of why someone would want to learn what is being taught. This can be done by considering the following questions, as if they were to be asked of the intended learner.

1 If you had a free choice, would you want to learn this?
2 If you don't want to learn this, why not?
  —It's a waste of time.
  —I'm not interested.
  —I've already done it.
  —I don't think it's relevant.
  —It doesn't concern me.
  —It won't help me.
  —I don't need this.
  —It's old fashioned.
  —I'm passed this stage.
3 If you do want to learn this, which of the following reasons are the most important? Rank them 1–9.
  —improve my performance.
  —increase my knowledge.
  —get promotion, or earn more.
  —just interested.
  —be better than colleagues.
  —do a more interesting job.
  —be more confident.
  —be less nervous.
  —it will help me.
4 What do you hope to have learned by the end of this training?

In a project I worked on, with a large UK building society, the new counter-top terminal system was intended, as far as mangement was concerned, to produce increased efficiency and reduce administration costs. When a representative group of staff were interviewed their learning needs had nothing to do with making the organization more efficient. Their needs were entirely personal, e.g. 'to do my job better', 'to provide customers with a good service', 'to be, and appear to be more modern and competent', 'to improve my job prospects', and so on.

By thinking about the proposed training in this way it is possible to develop a clearer view of how the prospective audience may be thinking about the training, and trainers can attempt to write the 'learning-need statement'.

The 'learning-need statement'

The 'learning-need statement' must cover three things:

- why the learner should want to learn this;
- the benefits from learning it; and
- the fun to be had while learning.

Very often learners are presented with an opportunity to learn that they have not sought. When this happens they will not have thought about their reasons for wanting to learn it. The learning statement can draw their attention to why they should want to learn this particular thing. This then puts them in a more positive frame of mind.

If there are no benefits to be had from learning, then why do it? The benefits should be expressed in personal terms. Few people are interested in the benefits that their learning will bring to the organization.

All learning should be fun. So why not let the prospective learners know how much fun it is going to be.

Here is an example 'learning-need statement'.

You may have noticed how tired you get, and how your shoulders, back and neck ache after a few hours working at your terminal. If you knew how to sit properly, and position your keyboard and screen, you would be able to feel more relaxed, and avoid the unnecessary aches and pains associated with terminal work. The short training course 'Sit Well, Be Well', will help you to feel more comfortable and relaxed at work. You will also have a lot of fun on the course, as you help to position other people, and to discover things about your body you probably won't believe.

If when people read this statement they feel they would like to go on the course, then it has worked. It might sound like a sales plug for the course, but then after all, that's exactly what it is.

There is no mention of increased productivity, or less time off sick, or better quality work. None of these will particularly interest the learner, no matter how much trainers would like to think they will; in fact stating these as objectives may have exactly the opposite effect.

A learning statement should give prospective learners a clear, interesting, and attractive view of the training *from their perspective*. This is very important to the design of the whole training programme. Trainers should constantly keep referring to the learner's perspective. After all it's not what the trainers want that matters. It's what the learners want, and unless they think they are getting it, they will switch off.

Stimulating learning-desire

Have you ever sat at the beginning of a training course full of excitement and anticipation? Well, if not quite that, what about waiting expectantly for it to begin? The speaker appears, introduces himself, and then proceeds to explain what the course is about, in terms of what he is going to say and do. Here is an example of an opening speech:

'Good morning. My name is David Smith, and I am going to tell you how to sit properly. I am going to demonstrate how to sit, and then I will explain the effects of poor sitting on the body . . .

Who cares what he's going to do. If I'm in the audience what I want to know is what I am going to do.

This kind of opening hardly stimulates learning-desire. If my learning need is strong enough I may stick with it, and I may enjoy it, and learn. But what a shame that the initial desire to learn is dampened so quickly.

What every training programme needs is an opening which immediatley re-kindles the desire to learn that brought the learners to attend the course, or start the programme. Here is an example:

'Good morning, my name is Brian Charles, and I want to start today by finding out why you've come. Who would like to start?'

or

'Good morning, my name is David Cross and I would like to explain what you will be offered the chance to do over the next two days. We hope to offer you the opportunity to explore . . .

This approach immediately draws attention to the audience's needs, i.e. the reasons they are there. It will involve the audience, and put the whole programme into their perspective.

To ensure that a training programme stimulates learning-desire, and maintains that stimulation it has to be designed on the principle of feeding learning. If trainers believe that training is the process of 'helping people to learn', then they have to construct training to do exactly that. The keys to stimulating learning-desire are:

- *exciting curiosity*
- *inviting involvement*
- *challenging perceptions*
- *feeding questioning minds*

Trainers have to provide the opportunity for learners to *explore and experiment.* They have to *remove fear and embarrassment,* and create a *safe and fun-filled environment.* So how can this be done? Trainers can start by listing each of the above keys to stimulating learning-desire, and then for each one state how they are going to achieve it in their training programme. If they relate this analysis to their list of key learning points, then they have the basis for developing an effective training programme.

In a major project in a UK company involving the training of hundreds of people in the use of a new system, the learning-desire of the group was stimulated and maintained by creating the learning environment described below.

The room was set out with a series of tables upon which we stood the new computer terminals. These were all covered with sheets (exciting curiosity). Chairs were set out in the middle of the circle of tables. We started by asking the group what they hoped to learn and how they were feeling (inviting involvement). The general feeling was one of apprehension. We challenged this by indicating that what they were going to learn was very easy, and that if everyone wasn't very happy within a short time we would delay implementation of the new system (challenging perceptions). We then asked what they wanted to know about the new system. We were able to give specific information to answer their questions (feeding questioning minds).

Next we showed the group a TV set, a tape recorder, and a typewriter, and asked them what they were, and whether they could use them. We then played a game. People chose to be a TV, or a tape recorder, or a typewriter. We then asked them to form three groups representing each machine and to present a short play that described what they were, and what they were used for (remove fear and embarrassment; create a safe fun-filled enviroment).

We then asked them if they wanted to see what was hidden under the sheets (exciting curiosity), and showed them the terminals. We invited them to switch on and to play with them (explore and experiment). After a short time we asked them to use a simple computer-based training package that described the new system, and gave them the chance to use it (inviting involvement).

The group were interested and involved from beginning to end, and their desire to learn was stimulated and maintained throughout.

Managing the learning process

Once the learning process starts it tends to gather a momentum of its own. If learning-desire has been sufficiently stimulated, then it can be left to the learners to do the actual learning.

Trainers do, however, still have to guide the learning process, ensuring that the things being learned are what they want to achieve. Keeping the programme on track is the objective of this section of learning-centred design.

The learning management process can be described as guiding a group of people across unfamiliar territory. There is a planned path, which the guides know, but the group don't. The journey starts and individual curiosity begins to lead down various side tracks. The guides want to encourage a certain amount of exploration, and they might even learn something themselves, but they have to bring the group back to the main path. Trainers need to build a number of points into their programme where they can pause and assess the direction the group are taking, and whether the learners are actually learning what they want to learn, and that this is what the trainers want them to learn.

The result of these pauses may be that trainers have to 'intervene' in the learning process that is taking place. This intervention should be as gentle as possible, and can often be successfully achieved by questioning the learners, rather than by directing them. It is much better to arrive at an agreement about which way to go, rather than giving an instruction as to which is the right way.

If the objective is to help people learn, then it is necessary to construct a training programme that does exactly that. This is far better achieved if trainers concentrate on establishing the learning needs of their audience, and then help them to meet them, than if they concentrate on their training needs.

Learning-centred design adds a new dimension to the initial analysis that precedes the building of training programmes. By thinking about the training programme from the point of view of the learner the emphasis has changed from 'training' to 'learning', and from what trainers want to achieve, to what they want the learners to achieve. This change of emphasis will considerably affect the way that trainers approach the building of the programme, and its subsequent success.

Learning-centred design is particularly important in the modern training environment, when more and more training is being delivered to learners via technology, and where learners have to be both self-motivated, and self-directed. If the training, in these circumstances, is not learning centred it will be rejected by the learners.

In high technology training far too much emphasis is placed upon what trainers think the audience need to learn. Because the subject matter is often highly technical and complex there is a mistaken belief that people need to learn by receiving and reacting to large amounts of information.

In a recent example this was proved to be untrue and indicated the importance of learning-centred design.

The project involved the need for a large number of people, several thousand, to learn to use a new system. The system used 24 screens and involved a series of complex procedures. The trainers had decided that a one-week training course should be run. It was going to take several months to train everyone, and hence to introduce the new system. I examined the system and then interviewed a group of potential users. I discovered that they already had a good understanding of their present job, but knew nothing about the new system. They clearly did not need to learn about the job, or about the system, but just how to do what they already were doing, but using the new system.

The training plan was changed and converted into a learning-centred approach where the job-related transactions were analysed, and a simple self-directed learning module produced for each transaction. The people did not have to learn *about* the system, but only how to use it, and not for every transaction, but only those that each individual carried out. The result was approximately two days' training per person, which was done in their own workplace, using a simple workbook, an audio cassette tape, and of course the system itself. The new system was implemented successfully in a matter of weeks.

By focusing on the learning process, and providing environments in which people can learn and grow, trainers are directly improving the potential for improved performance, and hence profits. Creating a learning-centred approach to training means providing learning opportunities and the appropriate environments, both on and off the job.

Key points

- People cannot be forced to learn, but they can be forcibly conditioned.
- Learning is voluntary.
- There are three crucial stages in carrying out learning-centred design:
  —defining learning needs;
  —deciding how learning-desire can be stimulated, and
  —managing the learning process.
- A learning-need statement should cover three things:
  —why the learner should want to learn this;
  —the benefits from learning it; and
  —the fun to be had while learning.
- A learning-need statement should give prospective learners a clear, interesting, and attractive view of the training from *their perspective.*
- The keys to stimulating learning desire are:
  —exciting curiosity;
  —inviting involvement;
  —challenging perceptions; and
  —feeding questioning minds.
- In addition to stimulating learning desire trainers need to:
  —provide opportunities for exploration and experimentation;
  —remove fear and embarrassment; and
  —provide a safe fun-filled environment.
- Learning management is a delicate process of guiding learners along the learning path without directing them, and allowing then a large degree of freedom.

11 Learning-centred design methodology

For many years I have tried to persuade trainers to use a structured approach for the production of effective learning-centred training materials. But which structure should be used? None of those that exist seems to fit my needs. What is needed is a methodology which will provide a basis for the analysis, design and development of learning opportunities that are based on the learning-centred design philosophy.

The need for a new methodology seems clear to me. If learning-centred training is to be designed and built it is essential to have a good knowledge and understanding of the learning that needs to take place. If, as I believe, it is not possible to determine the audience accurately, particularly in relation to their existing knowledge and skills, then a different approach has to be taken than has been used in the past. The reasons for this are as follows:

- it is not known what knowledge and skills each member of the audience may bring to the learning situation, and pre-tests do not in any way change this. To attempt to guess or make what seem like reasonable assumptions is pointless and only serves to limit the learning opportunity to a preconceived framework devised by the trainer.
- Training needs have usually been decreed from the organizational perspective, rather than from the learners' perspective. People do not learn for the organization; they learn for themselves.
- Key learning points have to be defined which meet the needs of the organization, but also meet the needs of the learners so that they will be motivated to learn. Getting this balance right is not easy, but unless it can be shown that there is a personal benefit from learning, people will quite simply just not learn.
- Throughout the design phase it is important to relate the material to the key learning points, constantly remembering that the learner will have choices about how this material is used. Decisions which are made about how the material is to be presented must cover a wide spectrum of possibilities.

This chapter is concerned more about the process involved and what is being achieved in each stage of the methodology, than about a presentation of the methodology itself.

The methodology provides a fully documented way of dealing with the largest of training problems. These are not encountered every day, and for many people the methodology will only be used in part, according to the precise needs that they have. The choice of what is appropriate for what purpose must be made by the user. Rules are ineffective when it comes to something as creative as producing training programmes, whether these are computer based or not.

The methodology is divided into three main sections, namely analysis, design, and development. Figure 11.1 shows the main elements of the methodology.

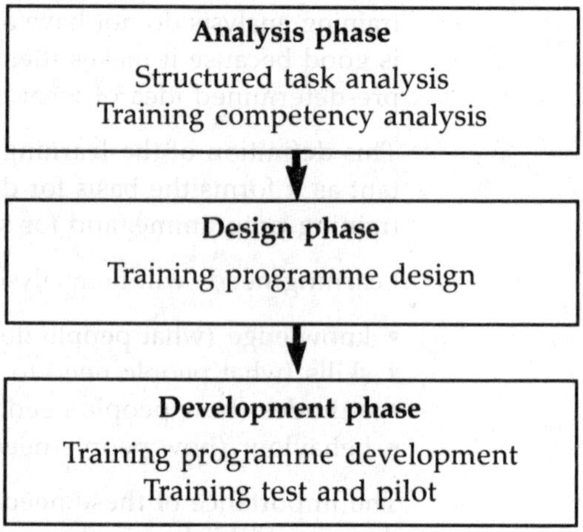

Figure 11.1 *Learning-centred design methodology*

Analysis

This phase is concerned with definition of the key learning points, and follows an approach very similar to the well-known structured task analysis. The knowledge, skills, attitudes, and behaviour needed by the learner to perform some pre-determined job are carefully analysed. From this analysis the key learning points are established. This leads into the preparation of a learning-needs statement which is written from the learner's perspective. The analysis process has four main aims;

- to produce a clear understanding of what has to be learned;
- to provide a schedule of things that will have to be learned by the target audience;
- to establish clear training objectives; and
- to provide detailed information on the subject matter content of the programme.

The analysis is also very important for deciding how to structure the training, both in terms of tutorials, simulations, practice, etc. The analysis section of the methodology is divided into two modules. These are;

- Structured task analysis
- Training competency analysis

Structured task analysis

The structured task analysis is divided into two main parts. The first of these is the breakdown of the job into the smallest possible elements, or transactions that take place. The purpose of this is to enable analysts to establish exactly what the user has to know and be able to do, in order to perform satisfactorily. In addition to this it provides a logical and sequential view of the job, and this helps the analyst to put the training into a logical and meaningful structure.

The first step in developing any training is to get a clear understanding of the problem/subject for which training is needed. Such an understanding can be gained by dividing the problem/subject into its component parts, and for each part analysing what needs to be learned. This is often a valuable learning process for training analysts. The fact that the training analysts do not have any existing knowledge of the subject matter is good because it makes them approach the learning needs without a pre-determined idea of what people will already know, or be able to do.

This definition of the learning that users will need to do is very important as it forms the basis for deciding the key learning points for the training programme, and for setting the training objectives.

Learning needs will be analysed into four categories:

- knowledge (what people need to know);
- skills (what people need to be able to do);
- attitudes (how people need to think); and
- behaviour (how people need to act).

The importance of these needs will be linked to the performance targets that are established in the next module. This means that in order to perform a certain task to the required level individuals will need to know and be able to do certain things, and think and behave in a certain way.

The outcome of the structured task analysis is a list of the learning requirements for each task, and a statement of training objectives.

Training competency analysis

This module seeks to define the performance standards expected of people who have completed the training. This is done by looking at each part of the job and deciding how competence is to be measured, and defining the criteria that are going to be used to assess competence.

It is important to analyse competency, otherwise there is no way in which the effectiveness of the training can be evaluated. I believe that it is important for people to demonstrate competency through practical exercises, rather than through examinations or knowledge tests.

Training competency analysis is concerned with establishing the performance objectives and criteria that will enable competence to be measured, both during and at the end of the training, and subsequently during normal working.

Most of the information that is needed for the analysis stage will come from observing the job and from discussions with competent people already doing the work. There is a lot of detailed information to collect, and one of the prime roles of the methodology is to provide a means for this to be documented in a suitable way so that it can be referred to when needed.

For many people detailed analysis seems tedious and time-consuming, and it becomes very easy to skimp on the gathering of information, or to make assumptions about the meaning of something instead of taking the effort to ask the appropriate person, or simply to forget to do something. Another of the roles of the methodology is to act as a guide and checklist through the analysis process, thus helping analysts to do a thorough job.

One of the questions people ask when using the methodology is 'Why is there so much copying from one form to the next?'. What this tells me is that the questioner has failed to grasp the purpose of the methodology. The *purpose* is not to fill in forms, although this happens. The purpose is to think about the job that is being analysed.

This process of constantly re-thinking about what is being done is what is meant by analysis. Those who see it as duplication are form fillers—certainly not analysts.

If the analysis is done carefully and thoroughly it will make the subsequent design and development stages much easier than would otherwise have been the case. It is very tempting to try to speed up the analysis process by not working at a detailed level, but the result of this is that training analysts end up not really knowing what they are talking about, hardly a recommendation for a trainer.

The outcome of the analysis process is a detailed record of the information needed to understand the job and/or the subject, and a complete set of documents to be used in the design phase.

Design

If the analysis process is about finding out what people need to learn, and researching the detailed information necessary to establish clear objectives, then the design phase is about deciding the best way for people to do the learning, i.e., devising the learning path.

The aims of design are threefold:

- To decide how the *key learning points* are to be covered in the training.
- To determine the format and sequence of the training.
- To select the best approach to the training, including the most appropriate media to use.

The design process is covered in one complete module which starts with a review of the *key learning points*, and how they can be approached, and then moves on to the structure and sequence of the training programme. This is followed by preparing an overview of each part (segment) of the training, after which the appropriate media can be selected. The end result of the process is the preparation of a training design report.

The design process calls for considerable imagination and innovation on the part of training analyst/designers. The methodology supports this freedom by providing a basic means of documenting ideas. The completion of the forms will not in itself produce good training. The forms are merely a means of guiding people through the process. Good training has two key elements. First is the way that the training enables learners to cover all the *key learning points* in a sensible and logical sequence. Second is the way in which the training gives the learners choice, and constantly motivates them to want to learn. Both of these elements depend on skill and experience.

This is the stage that training analyst/designers seem to look forward to most. This is the time when individual flair, imagination, and innovation come to the fore. So why on earth is it necessary to have documents to complete? How can this help designers with their thinking and problem solving? The answer is a great deal.

The mental process of thinking and problem solving is still a complete mystery. What we do know is that it happens at both the conscious and unconscious levels, and at speeds that confound even the fastest computers. What we also know is that this process is very easily distracted, especially in a busy working environment. Nor is it easy for people to lie on their desks with their eyes closed in deep thought without attracting unfriendly comments.

One way that we can assist this important process is by dealing with the problem in easily definable stages and recording the outcomes of each stage. In the design module of the methodology this is done by looking, or perhaps re-looking at the problem in the form of the key learning points. Then designers look at how they might deal with these in what seems like a logical sequence of interrelated segments, bringing into play all the knowledge and experience they have about learning methods. This causes them to think about how they might like to learn these things themselves and in which sequence it would make sense to them. This leads in turn to an idea of the programme which is called the outline. This can be drawn in the form of a flowchart to see if it does link and make sense.

Designers might now pause and rethink what their programme is looking like, and invariably they will makes changes and additions. They might even have a blinding flash of inspiration (the result of the hard work their subconscious mind has been doing). Whatever happens the programme will have a shape, an outline that can be visualised.

The third stage of the design process is to put some flesh onto the skeleton that has been produced, and in the methodology this is done by looking at each segment in turn. Each key learning point is reiterated (this is not duplication, it is a form of memory jogging and a means of concentrating thought). Then designers decide the best way they can imagine meeting these learning needs and covering the content of the segment. They are, if you like, problem-solving segment by segment.

The next task, usually when all the segments have been worked through, is to check the way in which the segments link together. This involves checking the structure and sequence. Of course designers will make more changes, and they may even have to go back and rethink the content of one or more segments. Finally when they are happy with the shape and content of the programme they can select the methods and media that they want to use to present/deliver the training.

By taking this step by step approach it is possible to convert one very large training problem into several much smaller and more easily solved problems. It is also much easier to see how the key learning points can be assessed segment by segment, and how exciting, highly motivating programmes can be designed. Designers often get stuck in ways of solving similar problems. Some trainers always think in terms of CBT, others in terms of courses, and yet others in terms of video. The best way to look at the approach is to have a completely open mind, and to let the design process flow smoothly through the stages described. The outcome of this can be both practical and exciting.

There are many trainers who feel that their experience is such that they don't need to follow a 'structured' process. Whether they know it or not they do follow exactly such a process, but it is a hidden one, the result of years of conditioning to do things a certain way. It always takes them down the safe well-trodden path. They never explore or try anything new, documentation is minimal, and the end result is often rigid and mediocre. It is not the use of a methodology which causes this, but rather the rigidity of thinking.

The outcome of the design process is a solution to the training problem and the framework for the building of an appropriate training programme. This is all contained in a training design report, which can be used as a customer sign-off document, and which is a blueprint for the building of the training programme.

Development

When the training programme has been designed and the training design report approved the development can commence. The development stage has three primary aims:

- To produce the specifications and definitions to be used by the programme producers, i.e. the content for video, CBT, etc.
- To clarify and set out the detailed content necessary to meet the key learning points segment by segment.
- To make any necessary amendments to the structure and content of the programme.

There are two modules in the development phase: these are the development itself, and the test and pilot of the finished programme.

Development

The development module of the methodology moves from the training design report to the completion of detailed specifications for the production of each segment of the programme. This involves looking carefully at the segment outlines and the training method and media, and writing the material appropriately. This cover the writing of the content of each segment, and the preparation of specifications for tutorials, exercises, simulations, and assessments.

The main aim is to provide the training producers with all the information they need to build what is required. Most training programmes use a variety of ways of meeting the learning needs. These can include: explanation, demonstration, exercises, games, simulations, and practice, and will thus use all the documents in the development module. The storyboard is particularly useful for describing shots for video, tape slide, windows to appear on screens for CBT, and the action needed to move through the tutorials.

Once again the decision of what documents are useful must lie with users. There are so many possible combinations of training problems that it is hard to lay down rules about which forms should be used. However, the documents provided should cover all possible needs.

The material should be written so that it can be passed on to the specialist production people with no danger of their misinterpreting what is required. This is helped if training analyst/designers follow the writing standards which form a separate part of the methodology (see the next chapter). The outcome of this module is a training programme specification containing all the information needed for the building of an effective training programme.

There is no module for production. Individual production specialists have their own approaches to how they go about their work. If the instructions and information they are given are clear and well documented then there should be no excuse for their not achieving the highest quality.

Test and pilot

The development is not complete until the programme has been tested and piloted. This module of the methodology provides a basic approach for carrying out and documenting these tasks. Basic documents are provided for planning tests, and for reporting on both tests and pilots. The forms can be seen as checklists for what is a very important process, which unfortunately is all too often ignored, or short circuited.

The methodology provides all the guidance, checklists, and basic documentation that experienced training analyst/designers should need for the most extensive training problem. In time, with repeated use, people will develop a way of using the methodology that will help them to produce outstanding work that is consistent, well documented, learning centred, and above all effective in achieving the training objectives.

Reactions to the methodology

When people are first introduced to the methodology they react in a wide variety of ways, from rejecting it outright, to accepting it as the answer to all their prayers. Neither of these extremes will benefit the individual or the organization.

Learning-centred design methodology has been developed to cater for a very wide scope of potential training problems. In the introduction to the methodology I suggest that people should learn to use the methodology with 'imagination and common sense'.

Here are a few thoughts about the methodology, from people using it:

'People do not like changing personal work styles that have been 'successful' and feel safe.'

'Discipline is seen as a contradiction to creativity.'

'Following a methodology seems time-consuming and cumbersome.'

'Creativity and initiative in using a methodology is far more effective than filling in the paperwork.'

'A methodology is a guide to the thinking process. It is a tool to help with analysis, and a basis for producing reports and information for others, i.e. a form of documentation.'

A standard, integrated, consistent approach to doing things enables high standards to be achieved without reducing personal freedom, creativity, or initiative.'

'Change means taking risks, but leads to high quality results.'

Learning-centred design methodology has been designed to cope with the most complex training design and development imaginable. The only time I have used every part of the methodology was when I had to design and develop a complete training programme for an organization from induction, through supervisory skills and management skills up to and including strategic management. The project was scheduled to take three years, had 150 modules and employed twelve staff. Without the methodology I would have been in a mess, there would have been no consistency, and I have no idea how I would have managed the project.

On the other hand if it is obvious to me that I don't need to use parts of the methodology, i.e. where I have the necessary information, then I only use the parts that are appropriate for the job I am doing. I do, however, always use certain parts of the methodology, even for the simplest of jobs. To do otherwise would be foolhardy. No matter how much experience I may have I still need to make sure I cover the basic essential ingredients.

The idea that the methodology is time-consuming and cumbersome comes from people not deciding how they could use it to help them produce good training. When time and money are limited the methodology is invaluable in ensuring that no time is wasted. I find that when I have only got a few days to complete some work, and I try to do it without the methodology, which I do from time to time, I get in a muddle, and after wasting a couple of days I return to the methodology, and I finish the work easily and quickly.

All trainers want to be able to use their own individual approach to how they do things. They all develop a style. I believe that when the methodology is used with imagination and common sense it enables trainers to desplay their style, and to release their creativity in the most productive way.

The principle underlying the design of the methodology is that tackling large problems is made easy by breaking the problem down into manageable components. The whole approach is, therefore, to take the job that someone has to learn to do, and break it down step by step into the smallest units possible, so that simple, short training programmes can be designed, with clear unambiguous and measurable objectives.

Extensions to the learning-centred design methodology

In Chapter 16 several new training tools are examined. One of these is embedded computer based training (ECBT) which in particular calls for some additions to the learning-centred methodology already described. This is because more detail is needed about specific elements of the computer system being learned, and there is a need for the writing of text to be embedded into the computer system.

The methodology for ECBT follows the same basic approach as the learning-centred design methodology, i.e. analysis, design, and development, but has some differences as described below.

ECBT analysis

The analysis process has four main aims:

- to produce a clear understanding of the way the target system is going to be used;
- to provide a schedule of things that will have to be learned by users;
- to establish clear training objectives; and
- to provide detailed information on the screens used in the system, and the conversion of this into Help information that is to be 'embedded' in the target system.

To achieve these aims the analysis process has been divided into two modules:

- Structured task analysis (this is basically the same process as used in learning-centred design methodology, but has an additional task as described below), and
- Screen definition

Structured task analysis

The additional outcome of the module is the preparation of a view of the system that will be used in the training screen definition. The overall aim is to gain a clear understanding of the job being carried out, and the way the system affects the job. This is then converted into clear training objectives, with the emphasis on how individuals should learn to use the system to perform their job more effectively.

Screen definition

This module of the analysis section is used to develop the Help information that is to be 'embedded' in the target system, and to advise the system designers on the form of the user interface. It involves analysing each screen used in the system, defining the use of the screen, all the fields on the screen, and the possible error conditions. This information is needed so that Help messages can be defined and written that cover every possibility, and which relate to the context in which the screen is being used. This module involves a considerable amount of work, because each screen has to be understood in its entirety.

The outcome of this module is a quality assurance document which contains the Help information that has been written for each screen in that part (activity) of the system. This document is checked by the systems and users group who then sign it off, after which the Help text is transferred to the Help database.

This analysis is completed before the training design is started so that the training analysts are aware of what information is going to be available from the system. This will in turn affect the way that they design the training tutorials and simulations. For example, if comprehensive Help is provided when errors occur then it is not necessary to train people in error correction procedures. If they do make an error they will get all the information they need to correct it from the system.

ECBT design

This is the same process as in the learning-centred design methodology, and has exactly the same objective of producing an outline training programme. It also seeks to identify clearly the places where system simulations should be included in the design.

When a system simulation is used a comprehensive database is needed. This module provides the basis for analysing the data that is needed on the database, or entered during the simulation. When the analysis is completed the way data is used in the simulations will be understood, and it will be possible to build them successfully.

ECBT development

This is the same as learning-centred design methodology. There is also an extensive set of standards for writing Help messages, which are contained in an appendix to the methodology. This set of standards is additional to the standards for writing training materials contained in learning-centred methodology.

Conclusion

Learning-centred design methodology has been designed to stand alone as a complete guide in itself for all forms of training. The standards included in the methodology are intended to have wide application throughout all aspects of the design and development of effective learning-centred designed training materials.

No methodology can ever be perfect. This is certainly true of the learning-centred design methodology. However, it has been used successfully and is based on the practical experience of producing effective learning-centred designed training programmes, including those for use in high technology training.

The end result of the methodology is an effective training programme that meets the key learning points, and does so without limiting the trainer's scope to design an exciting and enjoyable learning opportunity. Creativity and imagination are important factors in producing training that harnesses the learning-desires of the target audience. This can be done in a wide variety of ways, and individual trainers will want to exercise their own experience, flair and style. Even so it always helps to be able to work within a flexible structure and with a measure of guidance.

Key points

- Audiences of learners cannot be accurately defined in terms of attributes.
- Attempts to guess or make assumptions about an audience's attributes only serves to limit the learning opportunity to a preconceived framework devised by the trainer.

- Key learning points must meet the needs of the organization, and the needs of individuals.
- Learning-centred design methodology is divided into three phases and several modules as follows:

—analysis	—structured task analysis;
	—training competency analysis;
—design	—training programme design;
—development	—training programme development; and
	—training test and pilot.

- Structured task analysis is used to define the key learning points, and to gather subject matter information.
- Training competency analysis seeks to define the performance standards that are expected of people who have completed the training.
- The design phase is deciding the best way for the learners to do the learning, i.e. defining the learning path.
- The outcome of the design phase is a training design report.
- The development phase produces the detailed specifications for the building of the training programme.
- The principle underlying the design of the methodology is that tackling large problems is made easy by breaking the problem down into manageable components.

12 Writing standards for training materials

Introduction

These standards have been produced for use in conjunction with the learning-centred design methodology. The problem with producing any set of standards is selecting the best possible approach, which is both comprehensive and easy to follow. In these standards one overriding rule has been adopted. This rule requires people to keep everything they write small, short and simple. The intention is not to impress people with literary style, nor to write an Agatha Christie novel full of twists and turns and surprises. The job is to get a crisp message across to learners so that they can understand, remember, and recall the knowledge presented.

Training material should be interesting and should switch on the learning mechanisms of the reader. It should be attractively presented and feed the learner's curiosity. Learning is voluntary. People learn best when they *want* to discover and experiment.

Principles of writing training materials

Objective

The primary objective of all training material is to provide a means whereby learners can acquire the knowledge and skills required, easily and quickly.

The approach: guidelines

There are several general guidelines that should be followed when writing training material. These are listed below, with a brief explanation.

- **Explain don't tell** It is important that learners feel they are extracting the meaning from the message using their own intelligence. This means that reasons must be given for any statements made.
- **The reader is *learning;* the author is not *teaching*** Learning is voluntary: learners can't be made to learn, they can only be encouraged to do so.
- **Don't patronize** To switch people off from learning it is only necessary to write patronizing comments such as, *'you did quite well; if you try harder you will do better next time'.*
- **Encourage, but don't flatter** People who are learning respond well to

encouragement, but frequently reject flattery. Saying *'your performance is above average'*, is far better than *'Oh well done, you really are going great guns'*.
- **Be positive: failure does not exist, only success** It is so easy to write things such as, *'your error rate is . . .'*, when it should be *'your success rate is . . .'*

These guidelines should be followed for all kinds of training material; even when it is necessary to give instructions within an exercise it can be done following the guidelines.

When writing training material it is important to remember the basic approach to presenting training. There are six steps involved:

- Introduce the topic explaining what is being covered in this session.
- Write the content of the session.
- Summarize the material.
- If appropriate, demonstrate what has been explained.
- If possible, provide an opportunity to practise.
- Provide feedback on performance.

The approach: standards

In this section I am going to cover the basic standards that I believe should be applied to all training materials. The specific standards for writing screens, simulations and exercises, and demonstrations will be dealt with later. There are six main standards:

- short, simple words and sentences
- conversational language
- using the second person
- simple punctuation
- soft words
- affirmative and positive language

Each of these standards is explained below with a statement of the standard and the reasoning behind it.

Words and sentences

A considerable amount of research has been carried out to try to establish what makes the English language easy to read and understand. There are a variety of opinions, but the most commonly agreed elements of readable English are,

- short words
- short sentences

It is believed that, when reading, the brain works by recognizing and then interpreting each word in relation to visual images stored away in the memory. When this sentence is read: *'The large green tree has fallen on the car'*, the brain can visualize the scene because it has images in store that correspond to the words. The shorter the word the more likely it is to be in the store. The shorter the sentence, the easier it is to construct the appropriate scene. And because the words and sentences are both short the brain can carry out the process quickly. For these reasons it is believed that both the speed and the depth of understanding are enhanced.

In producing training material this is exactly the result to be achieved. This process can of course be short circuited by presenting the brain with the visual image itself, but more of this later.

Conversational language The use of conversational language is very effective in training materials. This is because the reader enters into the learning process rather than standing back from it. Of course it is not always possible to give the reader the opportunity to reply. Conversational language automatically forces writers to use short words and sentences, because the large majority of people talk in this way. It is also possible to use shortened words, such as *'shouldn't'* instead of *'should not'*. Here is an example of a piece of conversational language:

You should enter the customer's name and address first, before entering any other details. If you can't get the information from the customer you'll have to explain that without the information you won't be able to complete the transaction.

Second person The choice of second person is not difficult to understand. If the first person is used it sets the author up as the authority stating what should and should not be done. This generates a challenging atmosphere and reduces the reader's acceptance of what is being written. If the third person is used the material becomes remote, it neither seems to involve the author nor the reader. Here is the same example written in the third person.

'One should enter the customer's name and address first, before one enters any other details. The inability to do this will mean that the customer will have to be informed that the transaction is to be terminated.'

It is easy to see which approach is the most effective from a training point of view. The use of the second person in a conversational form is often challenged on the basis that it is incorrect grammar. If everyone were to write in strict accordance with the rules of grammar it could prevent the production of creative, meaningful and easily understood training materials.

Simple punctuation Punctuation is a system of symbols which enables the reader to recognize groups of words, and to identify the precise meaning and context of the words being used. In these standards only six punctuation symbols will be explained:

- The full stop or period
- The comma
- The apostrophe
- Parentheses or brackets
- Quotation marks
- Question mark

The effective use of these six symbols will give writers a considerable degree of flexibility in the way they write.

The full stop (.) is used in two ways:

- To end a group of words, usually signalling the end of a sentence.

- To signal an abbreviation.

The comma (,) is perhaps the most widely used punctuation symbol. In these standards I am concerned with seven main uses of the comma:

- When groups of words are joined with a conjuction, such as *and* and *but*, a comma should be used to indentify the conjunction. Here is an example:

  He walked along the ridge with powerful strides, but he was in danger of falling because his attention was on the circling bird.

- Where it is important to avoid misunderstanding, for example in written training programmes, the comma can be used when a sentence contains a list or series of elements. For example:

  He packed a waterproof jacket, several traps, ammunition, a first aid kit, and his pistol.

There are differing views on the use of the final comma before the *and*, which is known as the 'Oxford comma', and it is not universally used. There are of course cases where the final comma should always be used to avoid ambiguity. For example:

As he walked the hunter noticed the smooth grey of the beech stem, the silky texture of the birch, and the rugged pine.

If there is no comma after *birch*, the pine is given a silky texture.

- The comma is used to separate coordinate adjectives, i.e. adjectives referring to the same object.

  The warden was a strong, reliable, patient, and likeable leader.

- When a group of words are inserted into a sentence, that modify or add to the meaning, but do not change it, they are identified by placing a comma at the start and finish.

  The hunter, who was an excellent shot, took careful aim at the circling bird.

- The words *as* and *since* have a time meaning and a cause or reason meaning. These are distinguished by using a comma when a cause or reason is intended. Here is an example of each:

  The warden had not seen the hunter since the previous season.
  The climber slowed his precarious descent, as he felt in danger of falling.

- When words such as *therefore, however, for example,* and *consequently*, are inserted, they are identified by commas.
- Subordinate clauses and introductory phrases should be followed by a comma.

  Although he thought he knew where he was, the warden checked his position on the map.

  Realizing his mistake, the hunter lowered his rifle and moved to a new position.

The comma is used to bring clarity to the meaning of the words that have been written. If there is any doubt, the sentence can be tried with and without the comma, and the clearest one can be selected.

The apostrophe (') is used for two purposes:

- to define possession
- to indicate missing letters

Possession. An apostrophe is used when an *s* is added to a word to show possessive form; however, if the word ends in an *s* then only the apostrophe is added.

The warden saw the hunter's rifle.
He knew that hunters' rifles can only be confiscated in certain districts.

Missing letters. When letters are omitted in contractions, the place where the letter should have been is shown by an apostrophe, e.g. *hasn't* = *has not, can't* = *cannot, it's* = *it is.*

Parentheses or brackets ( ) are used to set off words inserted into a sentence, that are intended to supplement the content of the sentence.

Slowly (the terrain preventing his moving more quickly), the warden approached the hunter, who was by this time asleep.

Quotation marks ('. . .') are used to identify spoken or written words.

The warden approached the sleeping hunter. 'Stand up slowly, and throw your rifle to me', he said, loudly enough to wake the hunter.

Question mark (?) This should always be used at the end of a sentence which is a question. It replaces the full stop.

Soft words

When people read, though they might not recognize the cause, they sometimes feel that the style is harsh and grating. This is most likely due to the author's use of hard words. If soft words are used when writing, readers will find the message more acceptable.

Soft words are words which allow some option, some freedom of expression, and which seek agreement and support. Here are some example of hard and soft words.

Hard	*Soft*
When	If
Must	Should
Will	Could
Mistake	Error
Fault	Problem
Blame	Reason
Failed	Unsuccessful

Here are two examples, both give the same message, one using hard words, the other soft words:

When you make a mistake, or fail to complete the transaction, you must abort what you are doing. You must apologize to the customer and start again.

If you should encounter a problem, or be unable to finish the transaction, you should return to the beginning, explain to the customer, and try again.

The first is aggressive, gives no options, and apportions blame. It is harsh, and will increase, rather than reduce, the reader's fear of making mistakes.

Affirmative and positive language

In producing good training materials encouragement is a powerful motivator. It is likely, though research findings are not consistent, that if negative approaches are used, i.e. *what not to do*, learners may well not pick up the positive message that is intended.

Many humorous training videos follow this format, depicting all kinds of terrible consequences from doing the wrong thing. The opinions of trainers differ widely on this subject, but I believe it is better to be affirmative and positive in everything I write.

A great many people learn most effectively from observing and copying. How much better for them to observe and copy the right way to do things.

It is quite easy to ensure that writing is affirmative and positive, it simply means omitting the words *no* and *not* from what is written. If it is felt that this is going to limit what is written and the way it is written, then practice should prove the point one way or the other.

Here are three examples of negative language.

- You must not enter the customer's surname before the first name.
- If you try to enter brackets into the telephone number, you will find that the system will not accept them, and will reject the input with an error message.
- When opening a new account, you must not agree to the limit requested until you have checked the customer's credit worthiness.

All the above messages are correct in the information that they give to learners, but they have the effect of making learners feel that there are many things they can do wrong. The following are the same three messages written in an affirmative and positive way.

- You should enter the customer's first name before their surname.
- The telephone number field is a numeric field. If you enter brackets the system will reject your input and ask you to input numbers only.
- When opening a new account check the customer's credit before agreeing to the limit requested.

These three messages give exactly the same information, but do so in a way that makes learners feel more in control and, therefore, makes the messages more acceptable.

It may be noticed that in making the writing affirmative and positive the order of the words has changed, and that the number of words used is usually less in the affirmative and positive versions, which is another good feature of this style.

Simulations and exercises

Objective

The objective of this standard is to set out the recommended approach to the writing of simulations and exercises, which are in addition to all the preceding standards.

The purpose in writing simulations and exercises is to enable learners to practise, and gain proficiency, in a protected and supportive enviroment.

The approach: guidelines

To achieve these objectives we must produce simulations and exercises which learners can complete relatively easily. Trainers should also ensure that learners graduate from simple exercises to more complex ones as their confidence grows. It is appropriate at this point in the standard to give a definition of a simulation and of an exercise.

Simulation An exact replica of the situation the learner will meet in the working environment, or as near a facsimile as can be produced.

Exercise An opportunity to practise the application of knowledge, and the development of skills, in a way that does not exactly replicate the working environment.

There are three factors of paramount importance in producing effective simulations and exercises, and these are:

- conditions should be as close to reality as possible.
- Ambiguity of words and instructions should be strenuously avoided.
- If the training is computer based, there should be as much support as possible from the system.

The aim of simulations and exercises is to practise what has already been learned or to stimulate learning via experimentation and exploration. The key words from a learning point of view are: interest, challenge, confidence, competence, consolidation, reinforcement, and satisfaction. None of this will be achieved if trainers produce simulations and exercises that push learners too hard.

Successful simulations and exercises are highly interactive. The training programme and facilitators must be capable of responding, when there is a need, and when learners request it.

The approach: standards

In addition to all the preceding standards for writing training materials, which apply equally to simulations and exercises, there are three further standards, concerned with

- levels
- achievables
- problems

Levels There are four primary levels at which simulations and exercises can be written.

- Directed and controlled
- Directed and monitored
- Guided and monitored
- Free format and monitored

Directed and controlled This level requires learners to follow instructions, the responses to which are under the control of the training programme. This is the easiest form of exercise because learners are unable to do anything wrong.

Learners should know that they are working under the supervision of the training programme, and how the programme will respond to them.

The instructions should say what to do, and how to do it. Learners should then be able to carry them out. At this level only one instruction at a time should be completed. Patronizing comments such as *'Oh! well done'* should be avoided.

On completion, learners should receive information on how well the exercise went. The information should be accurate, simply stated, and both supportive and encouraging.

Directed and monitored Learners follow instructions as in the previous level, but now the simulation or exercise only monitors what happens. This means that as learners can make mistakes, the simulation must be written to respond appropriately when this happens.

An appropriate response to an error would be to provide learners with information on the cause of the error, and the action to take to correct it.

The simulation or exercise is monitored to provide information on learning performance, and other feedback as appropriate.

Guided and monitored The third level ceases to provide instruction, but provides guidance, either initiated or at the request of learners. The guidance given should be as brief as possible and relate to the two factors, what to do, and how to do it. Guidance will usually be necessary when an error occurs (initiated), or when learners get stuck (requested). This latter situation will call for some creative thinking on the part of the training analyst on when to provide such guidance.

The exercise will be monitored to provide information on when guidance was given and requested, as well as on the learners' performance. In the case of ECBT, guidance will mostly be provided by the Help facility embedded in the system.

Free format and monitored This is the fourth and highest level, and requires the training analyst to produce a simulation or exercise which doesn't provide any guidance, except in the case of ECBT for Help facilities.

Learners are presented with access to the simulation, and the data necessary to complete the work. If learners make any errors then they must correct them themselves, the only assistance being Help from the system. Learners should be given information about the simulation and the expected outcome. The work they do will be fully monitored, and in the case of ECBT this will include a record of the use made of Help.

The monitoring will provide information on performance, and include a comparison with the expected results.

Achievables

Before learners start a simulation or exercise, it is important that they are aware of the things they have to achieve. The simulation should, therefore, start with an explanation of the achievables, and a reiteration of the learning points being practised.

The recommended format of a simulation or exercise should be as follows:

- Introduction — stating the purpose of the simulation and the learning points to be practised.
- Achievables — the expected results, and the performance ratios to be achieved.
- Measurements — the way performance is to be measured.
- Simulation — the actual simulation.
- Data — the data required to complete the simulation.
- Results — the actual results achieved.
- Performance — a summary of the overall performance, and a comparison with the expected.

The achievables should be easy to understand and calculate, so that learners can relate the outcome to what they have just done. Subjective assessment is not necessary, as learners can do this for themselves.

Problems During a simulation or exercise learners may be working alone, or under supervision. Either way it is essential that a special tutur guide is produced to explain how to overcome problems that may be encountered. I believe that there are four major types of problem encountered by learners:

- using training materials
- making mistakes
- getting lost
- system failure

Using training materials Regardless of how careful trainers are in writing training programmes, the learners will still want to have a detailed explanation of what it is they are supposed to do.

This should be provided in the tutor guide, and cover:

- the materials involved
- the facilities needed
- the sequence of action
- signposts and checkpoints

Signposts point to where to go after each action, and checkpoints enable the learner to discover where they are.

Making mistakes If learners make mistakes, either the system or the training programme should respond with a carefully written message. The message should contain three elements: a simple description of the mistake; a definition of the cause; and the correction procedure. Cryptic error messages, e.g. *E1003 Mandatory field*, are not acceptable.

Learners should be given the opportunity of correcting the error and proceeding with the simulation. A speedy and effective response to errors is a sign of growing confidence. People are not afraid of making mistakes that they can easily correct.

Getting lost The use of signposts and checkpoints in the training programme should help learners to navigate through the simulation successfully. Even with such features it is still possible to get lost. When writing the programme trainers should consider how they are going to advise learners to react if they get lost.

There are three recommended ways to do this:

- Return to start and skip to last known position.
- Return to the last known position and restart.
- Request guidance on current position and continuation action.

System failure If the training programme is computer based, it is possible that the system may fail. If this happens during a simulation or exercise it will confuse learners and may well corrupt the data entered so far. It is unlikely that a situation where such failure will not occur can be created, so the best course of action is to provide information on recovery procedures in the tutor guide. The recommended way of doing this is to restart the system, i.e. re-boot, and start the simulation or exercise again.

Writing demonstrations

Objective This standard relates to the writing of demonstrations which are part of a training programme. The objective is to set out the way to write material which feeds the learner's observation faculty. Observation is one of the primary learning mechanisms, and should appeal to the curiosity that most people possess in abundance.

The approach: guidelines A demonstration contains three parts:

- description of the demonstration
- the demonstration
- confirmation of understanding

These three parts are written in such a way that the curiosity of learners is stimulated, then satisfied, and finally confirmed before they move on to practise.

The approach: standards It is particularly important when a demonstration is being written, that the writer is aware that learners are more concerned with visual perception than with reading. This means that the writer should concentrate on producing material which is visually descriptive, has impact, and is non-demanding.

The standards to observe deal with the three parts of the demonstration, as described above. All the preceding standards for writing training material apply to writing demonstrations. A demonstration may be displayed on slide, video, live presentation, or on a computer screen. Whichever medium is used the writing standards set out below apply.

Describing the demonstration In order to stimulate learners' curiosity the demonstration should be described in terms of what they are going to see, for example:

In this demonstration, you are going to see the way that data are entered into the system. The key points to watch for are:

- the way the cursor moves automatically from field to field
- the way that Help can be requested
- how errors are detected and Help given to correct them

The programme or trainer should inform learners what action, if any, they will have to take during the demonstration. Totally passive demonstrations are not necessarily the best approach.

The demonstration The demonstration should be written in a visual context, and the use of the storyboard approach is recommended. The key requirements are to describe:

- what to show
- how to show it
- learner reaction

What to show This should be set out in the logical sequence of the events to be displayed, and should be preceded by the expression, *show. . . .* Each item to be shown should be listed separately by the designer.

How to show it For each of the items to be shown state the way that it is to be shown. If, for example, one of the items to be shown was, *'show the correct input of the customer's name'*, then the description of how it was to be shown might read as follows, *'program the system to enter a customer's name into the appropriate field on the screen'*.

The demonstration is written as if it is being addressed to the producer of the demonstration, which is of course exactly what is happening.

Learner reaction When a reaction is called from learners, it has to be indicated in the demonstration by stating, for example, *'at this point invite learners to key in a name.'* In the demonstration itself this would appear as a simple request to learners, such as, *'please key in the name Trevor Bentley.'*

Confirmation of understanding It is likely that understanding will have to be confirmed by a simple summary of what has been demonstrated. The opportunity to question learners, either face to face, or by computer-based interaction is usually limited. In face-to-face it is limited by the constraints of all human interaction, in CBT it is limited by the software.

When questions can be asked, they should of the type, *'what did you see happen in respect to . . .?'* Not *'do you now know how to . . .'*

Conclusion

These writing standards have been devised to help trainers to produce effective training material. If they are found to hinder style, or restrict the effectiveness of the writing, then they should be used with common sense and imagination. Slavishly following rules does not normally work, but following standards that are understood, appreciated and respected normally leads to the production of better work. I hope these standards fall into this category.

Key points

- The job of these standards is to help to get a crisp message across to learners so that they can understand, remember, and recall the knowledge presented.
- Keep everything written small, short and simple.
- The purpose in writing simulations and exercises is to enable learners to practise, and gain proficiency, in a protected and supportive enviroment.
- Demonstrations feed the learner's observation faculty. Observation is one of the primary learning mechanisms, and should appeal to the curiosity that most people possess in abundance.

13 Training assessment and evaluation

Nothing seems to cause more concern and misunderstanding than the subjects of assessment and evaluation. I believe that this is because many people mix up two fundamental elements of training, namely the quality of the training that takes place, and the quality and value of the learning that results.

At a workshop in Australia when a group of trainers were asked to list all the factors that should be assessed to determine the success of a training event, the vast majority of the items listed were inputs to the training process, rather than learning outcomes. (see Figure 13.1)

It is important to measure both the inputs and the outputs of the training process. The inputs need to be measured so that the quality of the help that the learners receive can be assessed, and outputs so that the benefit the learners gain from the training can be evaluated.

Perhaps this topic can be best discussed by looking at the things that need to be assessed, and how these can be measured and evaluated. Figure 13.1 is a mind map of the two key aspects of inputs and outputs that I will use as a basis for the discussion. However, before I start this discussion I will give some simple definitions for the words 'assessment' and 'evaluation'.

Assessment The process of calculating the value of something. (Usually used in the context of assessing tax liability). The current use of the term would seem to indicate a broader definition would be appropriate, such as: A judgement or opinion as to quality in relation to a pre-determined scale.

Evaluation The process of ascertaining or fixing value or worth.

Assessment and evaluation in training can lead to the following possibilities:

- Trainers could assess fellow trainers on inputs to the training process. This would be affected by personal views on what constitutes good training.
- Learners could assess trainers on inputs to the training process. This would be influenced by how well learners related to the trainer, and how much they enjoyed the training.
- Learners could evaluate the worth of the training to themselves, i.e.

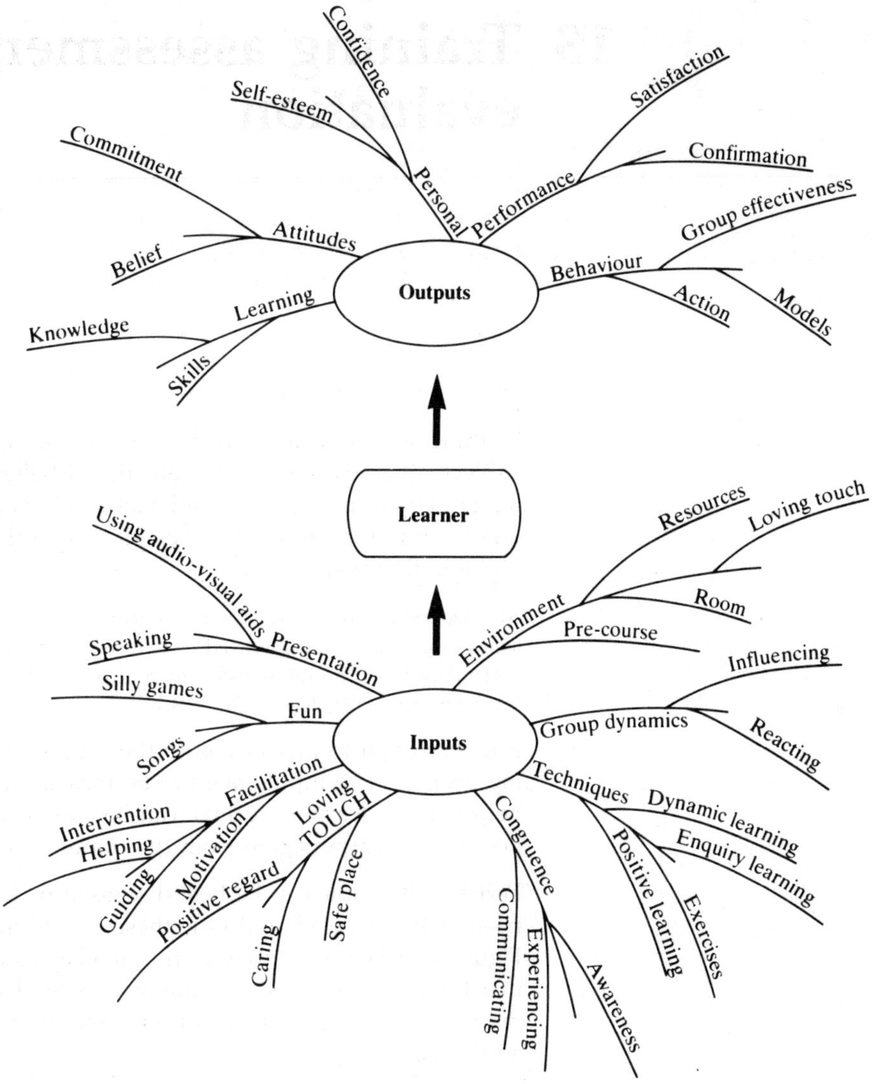

Figure 13.1 *Mind map of inputs to, and outputs from training*

the worth of the learning outcomes. This would be affected by many personal factors that would be different for every learner.

- The learners' sponsors could evaluate the worth of the training to their activity, and to the organization, i.e. the worth of the learning outcomes. This would be different for different sponsors, and depend on the working environment, and how well it supported the learner.

So it immediately becomes obvious that there is a problem in establishing any really meaningful assessment of training, or evaluation of learning outcomes. But perhaps it is incumbent upon trainers to try to find a way, whether subjective or objective, to evaluate the benefit of what can be a significant investment in time, effort and money.

Inputs to the training process

On the mind map I have divided the inputs into eight main branches: facilitation, fun, presentation, environment, group dynamics, techniques, congruence, and a loving TOUCH. This is not an exhaustive set of headings but suits my purpose here very well.

Facilitation

This is the process of helping people to do things for themselves without the facilitator appearing to have had anything to do with it. It covers the basic stages of helping, guiding, motivating and intervening with care and skill when necessary to keep learning on the right track, i.e. the track that the learners have decided they want to follow.

So how can facilitation skills be assessed except in a subjective way? And presumably they can only be assessed by participants. A list of items such as: directiveness, freedom, asking the group, intervention style, and so on, could be used and a score from 1 to 5 recorded. But is not the success of facilitation the outcome?

Fun

People learn and enjoy learning when they are having fun. Having fun is often associated with not being adult, as if being adult is the only desirable state. Singing songs and playing games is a glorious way to spend time getting to know people.

At a recent workshop someone wrote on a flipchart 'We should lighten the atmosphere by having fun, but without being silly.' I asked why they had suggested we should not be silly. There was no immediate response so I suggested that someone did something silly. What followed was a free expression of how people felt, with many people overcoming long-held conditioning and embarrassment.

People have been told so often as children not to be silly, that they think it is wrong to be silly. Sometimes it is wonderful to be really, really silly.

Can fun be assessed beyond a simple 'yes we had fun', or 'no we didn't have fun'?

Presentation

There will often be a need to present information to people in a clear articulate way that aids understanding. Being able to speak clearly and to present ideas graphically will always be essential tools of the skilled trainer. Though for me personally there are fewer and fewer occasions when I present, it is nevertheless a skill I am pleased to have developed.

Assessing presentation means making some subjective judgement of things such as: speaking voice, stance, use of humour, clarity, start, middle, end, and so forth. And usually the main value of this assessment is to help the trainer to improve, rather than assessing the audience's perception, interest, attention and understanding.

Environment

Understanding and creating learning environments are vital to providing really effective learning opportunities. The environment covers what is done prior to training, the physical facilities, the way resources are provided and used, and the psychological atmosphere created.

Assessing the environment is once again a subjective thing. If the question was asked, 'was the environment conducive to training?' the answers would vary considerably depending upon individual learners' preferences. A list of factors could be produced and scored, but I doubt if it would provide anything of value.

Group dynamics The way groups work together has always fascinated me, and I have been, and still am a student of group dynamics. It is a subject for which I don't believe there are any masters. With time and experience it becomes possible to observe and sense the way a group is working, and this sense helps the facilitator to know if and when to intervene in the learning process.

I have produced a list of key factors in group dynamics which I now use to assess trainers in my Trainer Training workshop. Here is the list of items I use:

Empathy Recognizing and responding to needs of others in the group.

Leadership Being willing and able to take the lead when you feel this is appropriate.

Listening Paying careful attention to what others are saying.

Assertiveness Being forthright in expressing opinions and making sure you are not dominated or controlled by others in the group.

Contributing Able to make valid and relevant contributions, and to remain silent when having nothing to say, i.e. not speaking for the sake of it.

Direction Being able to avoid being sidetracked and bringing the group back to the main direction.

Challenging Making contributions that challenge the perceptions and beliefs of others in the group.

Calming Being able to calm the ruffled waters without being patronizing, or stopping the flow of good ideas.

Influencing Having the ability to influence the direction of the group and to affect the perceptions and beliefs of others.

Techniques Knowing when to use the various training techniques to help learning take place is another important element of the whole process. Techniques such as: dynamic learning, enquiry learning, exercises, lectures, presentations, case studies, simulations, and so on. But how can the use of such techniques be assessed? Once again a list could be produced and scored, with items such as: techniques used, how well used, did they achieve their aim, level of interest, relevance to subject, and so on. Once again these are subjective views and will probably differ widely.

Congruence I believe that congruence is very important. It is concerned with the way the facilitator relates to the group, and they to the facilitator. Are they on the same wavelength? It covers such items as: awareness, experiencing, communicating, and sharing. It is perhaps one of the hardest factors to assess. If it is there it is felt; if it is not there it is not noticed, except for an unexplainable feeling of unease.

Loving TOUCH When I first introduced this idea to a workshop, several people thought

I was mad. 'What has this got to do with training?' they asked. I asked them to humour me, and by the end of the workshop they were convinced. TOUCH, as mentioned in Chapter 9 stands for trust, openness, understanding, confidentiality, and honesty.

With these in place congruence is much more possible, and people feel free to be themselves and to release their inherent learning skills. But can it be assessed? I am not at all sure that it can.

All the inputs can be listed and scored on a scale, but in the end what does it mean? If I had done this at one workshop I attended the score would have been very low, yet I have never before learned as much in so short a time. Such an experience makes me wonder if there is any real value in measuring inputs.

Outputs from the training process

In the mind map (Figure 13.1) I have shown five branches for the outputs: learning, attitudes, personal, behaviour, and performance. This is not an exhaustive list, but these are in my view the main outcomes of training.

Learning

In learning-centred training, the key learning points will have been clearly stated, and learners will have set down their own personal learning objectives. These will cover the acquisition of knowledge and skills, as well as attitudinal and behaviour changes. Evaluating learning can be done in three main ways, subjective opinion, tests/examinations, and exercises.

Subjective opinion leads people to examine what they believe they have learned from their own perspective. This can be checked with their peers, and/or with the facilitator. One very good way to do this is by a statement and demonstration of what has been learned.

Tests/examinations at best what we have here is a simple recall of information. If we want to test memory then this is a good way to do it. Some examiners think that understanding can be displayed by answering questions, but a good memory can make it *look* as if the person understands, whereas some people who do understand find it difficult to display this via a test. I don't use tests and examinations as I consider them counterproductive to enjoyable learning. This is because the knowledge that a test is involved places pressure and stress on the learner, which makes it hard to learn. People learn best when they want to, not when they are forced to.

Exercises these can be used to allow the learners to display what they have learned in a practical way. An exercise can include writing, talking, demonstrating, and doing things that clearly show learners have learned what was desired. If these are designed in an imaginative way, and if learners have access to all the information they need, then the exercises become learning opportunities as well as a basis of evaluation.

Attitudes

It is possible to evaluate the worth of attitudinal changes, from both the learners' and their sponsors' point of view. However, this needs to be done some time after the training has been completed. Oh, it is possible to check whether people believe they have made any shifts in thinking at the end of the training, but the real value comes if these changes stick and produce benefits for the learner.

Personal Personal benefits can come in all shapes and sizes, but perhaps the two most significant ones are confidence and self-esteem. Learners have to make their own personal evaluation of these factors, but it is possible for others to notice differences in the way learners act after the training. This is an area where coaching and counselling are valuable in maintaining the individuals' new-found confidence, which will of course affect performance.

Behaviour Apart from thinking differently, learners will probably also start to act differently, but this is another factor of learning that can only be evaluated some time after the training has been completed. Again it is useful if the working environment to which learners return is supportive, and encouraging. Coaching and counselling will help to maintain the learners' new behaviour—if it is favourable, of course.

Performance All the learning outcomes finally lead to improved performance, which is what makes the investment in training worth while. Improved performance can be evaluated, to a limited extent, during training via exercises, but the real evaluation has to take place in the working environment. Learners should be able to return after training and make their own evaluation. In addition the learners' sponsors should be able to measure improvements. For this to happen it will be necessary to have performance objectives which are clearly defined, and which can be measured easily by the performers, as well as by their supervisors. The training competency module of the methodology is used to establish performance targets, performance indices, and performance standards. With these in place it is possible to make a clear evaluation of performance improvements. Without them the evaluation will be subjective at best, and non-existent at worst.

Conclusion

Assessment of training inputs and the evaluation of learning outcomes (training outputs) are quite different things. A training programme which is highly rated in terms of inputs may have poor learning outcomes and vice versa. This is because of the totally unpredictable impact of human relationships and personalities that take place in all learning environments. Even when the relationship appears to be between people and machines, it is in fact between the learners and the designers of the computer-based learning programme. People will learn in almost any environment if they want to, and they will make use of what they learn if they want to. If people don't want to learn or make use of their learning there is very little anyone else can do about it. Whether or not the assessment of inputs is good and the learning outcomes are excellent, it still depends totally on the individual learner whether or not the learning is converted into improved performance.

Key points

- There are two fundamental elements of training, namely the quality of the training that takes place, and the quality and value of the learning outcomes that result.
- Assessment is judging the quality of something.
- Evaluation is ascertaining the value or worth of something.
- Learning inputs cover facilitation, fun, presentation, environment, group dynamics, techniques, congruence, and a loving touch.
- Learning outputs cover the learning that takes place, attitudes that result, personal benefits, behaviour, and performance. This is not an exhaustive list, but are in my view the main outcomes.
- It is suggested that learning inputs can be assessed, and learning outputs evaluated.

PART FIVE

Training environments

14 Continuous training and support

Changes take place so rapidly that within a few years the knowledge and skills acquired from extensive training is obsolete, and people have to retrain. This need for continuous training and support in the workplace is going to increase.

Up to the present time people have been accustomed to seeing training as a spasmodic 'off the job' activity, linked to an unstructured 'on the job' task. I say unstructured, because little if any effective training takes place on the job, though a good deal of learning is done. People learning often work with someone who can 'do' the job. They learn extremely well from observation and questioning, but what do they learn? They learn how the people they are observing do the job, not necessarily how the job should be done. Here is a specific example of this happening.

In the subsidiary of a large Australian company a learning-centred approach was being developed. One person who had had a particularly authoritarian background could not escape from the content-centred teaching approach. This person did not use the learning-centred approach, and within a short time the staff working with this person were similarly affected in their attitudes to the learning-centred approach. They had not been 'trained', but they had learned from the example of their supervisor.

What is needed is some means whereby individuals can receive continuous updating and training, when they need it, when they ask for it, and delivered to them in their workplace. This can be provided by supervisors, more experienced colleagues, or via the technology they use in their daily work.

People who achieve very high levels of performance, athletes for example, train continuously in order to reach their peak, to maintain themselves at their peak, and to expand their capabilities to new levels of achievement. What happens when they let up on their training, or stop altogether? They quickly fall below their previous performance levels.

Perhaps this is not the level of achievement and commitment being aimed for, but people are probably concerned to see that they are able to perform to the best of their abilities and to maintain and improve their performance if possible.

Continuous training

Continuous training is a three-stage process of learning, practising, and reviewing performance. It should not stop. People should not reach a satisfactory level and switch off, because like the athlete their performance will deteriorate. Continuous training is an investment in performance.

For most people this process only works if they have targets to aim for. These targets must be related to their current level of knowledge and skill and must be based on realistic levels of expectation.

All three stages of the process are vital elements of success, but perhaps the most critical element is the review. This is always difficult for both the reviewer and the person being reviewed. No one responds with pleasure to criticism, and yet unless people accept and understand the outcome of the review they cannot improve. Everyone has been conditioned to love praise and to feel bad about criticism, but if criticism is properly and positively delivered people learn from it. People don't learn from praise, but learning and performance are reinforced by it.

The review must tell people three things:

- how they are performing—preferably in relation to some predetermined and measurable standard;
- why they are performing at that level; and
- what action they can take to improve.

The review is usually followed by more learning, then by a period of practice at what is hoped is an improved level of performance. This process should never stop. People may change direction, add new skills; they may grow both in the level and extent of their performance, but they should never stop the development process. However, for many people the process does stop. *Why?* Some of the reasons could be:

- personal desire to stop—give up
- the process itself stops
- personal refusal to follow the process
- motivation is lacking
- opportunity is not available
- individuals decide they have reached the peak

If organizations can provide the infrastructure to maintain this continuous development process and provide the motivation through self-generated learning, practice and review, then there should be significant improvements in performance.

When the need for continuous training services is related to the use of high technology in the workplace, it can be seen that a facility is required which is permanently available to the user. This facility must do three main things. It must measure performance; assess what the measurements indicate; and then lead directly on to coaching so that performance can be improved.

Measuring performance

Several critical questions need to be answered before performance can be measured. These are listed below:

- What index of performance is appropriate?
- What is going to be measured?
- How is it going to be measured?
- What standards are being aimed for?
- How are the standards set?
- Who should be involved?

What index of performance is appropriate?

In using a computer system, particularly when inputting data, accuracy becomes very important. If accuracy is used as an example of measuring performance, both the number of errors and the value of errors might be measured, but in relation to what? Perhaps the total number of transactions and the total value of transactions. These should be expressed in a positive way so as to report success rates, not error rates.

If the number of correct transactions is taken in relation to the total number of transactions it becomes an index of performance, which might be called the 'success volume index'. The value of correct transactions in relation to the total value of the transactions might be called the 'success value index'.

These indices need to be agreed with the people whose performance is being measured.

What is going to be measured?

Once the index is agreed the criteria that are going to be measured can be decided. In the above example the criteria would be:

- volume of correct transactions
- value of correct transactions
- volume of transactions
- value of transactions

How are the criteria going to be measured?

It can be done continuously, or a sample can be taken of the individual's activity. It is what is practical in relation to the benefit that is important. Can the occurrence, type, value and volume of errors be logged? Can the volume, type and value of transactions be logged? If it can be done, then how? If it can't be done then criteria must be found that can be measured and the performance index will have to be re-examined.

What standards are being aimed for?

This is, very often, one of the most difficult things to decide. There might need to be more than one standard to deal with different levels of performance. In the example the levels might be as shown in Table 14.1.

Table 14.1 *Performance standards*

	% by volume	*% by value*
Novice	90	95
Competent	95	98
Expert	98	99

It may be more appropriate to set a range within which the result index must fall, e.g. 85–95 per cent.

How are the standards set?

The usual ways are: guesswork, experience, measurement, and agreement. Whichever method is used it has to be possible to adjust the standard depending upon what is learnt when performance starts to be measured.

Who should be involved?

There are three groups involved in establishing the criteria and standards for measuring performance:

- the individuals being measured
- their supervisors
- their manager

Training analysts can make suggestions, but shouldn't make decisions about performance criteria and standards.

Once the key questions have been answered the monitoring system can be constructed. Ideally it should be possible to monitor the activity of the individual both while undergoing training and while working with the system.

Assessing performance

Assessing the performance of people working with high technology presents the usual problems associated with measuring human performance. The technology itself can help, but it does not replace the need for careful analysis of the job and the work the person is doing.

Performance assessment has three main steps:

- Measure result
- Interpret meaning
- Determine action

It is dangerous to make assessments too precise. There will be many factors involved that will need to be explored. Such factors as the working environment, the complexity of the system, the quality of the screen design, are just a few that have to be considered.

A system can be built to measure and give a suggested reason for any deviation and propose corrective action, but this facility has to be used carefully. In a self-assessement process individuals can determine their own reasons, take appropriate action, and then input their reasons to complete the training record.

The performance of high technology workers can be assessed in two main areas:

- use of technology
- use of the application

Use of technology

This might be measured by speed of imput and/or incorrect key strokes. In addition it might be appropriate to log the way the system is used, i.e. navigation between menus and screens. The measurement could lead to suggestions for specific forms of training, such as keyboard dexterity. This area is not a major one for performance improvement except where the application system requires intensive or high volume work.

Use of application

This is a much more important area and is related to:

- use of the system, i.e. the user's response to the system
- job activity, i.e. the way people use the system to do their jobs.

The first of these is the easier to measure and interpret. The second is often a problem depending upon the job and the application system.

When performance has been measured and assessed it has to be recorded and communicated to the individual, with or without interpretation. The response from the individual should be a desire to seek an appropriate interpretation and then to act to obtain more training to improve performance.

The action individuals take could be via the system or via their supervisor. Whichever route is followed there needs to be some control over people's time and use of the system.

Coaching

Trainers have different ideas about what coaching is. It might be useful if I offer a definition: *Motivating, encouraging and helping an individual to improve performance.*

Coaching consists of the following key activities:

Measuring This activity has already been discussed, but it is worth repeating that the basis for measuring performance must be agreed and accepted by the person being measured.

Observing In the high technology environment a good deal of the watching can be carried out by the system. The observation has to be informed and this opens the door for the application of expert computer systems.

Reasoning This stage is concerned with working out the possible reasons for the level of achievement measured, bearing in mind the information from the observation stage.

Encouraging Relaying the information on performance in a positive and encouraging way:
SUCCESS RATE = 89%, *not* ERROR RATE = 11%

Guiding Showing and explaining how the success rate can be improved, suggesting certain changes in practice, or prefered methods to be followed.

Operating People have to carry out the task for which the performance is being measured. They must perform.

When measuring performance it is not only to establish where performance is below par, it is also to discover where performance is above the required level and to identify *high performers.*

High performers can then be monitored and trainers can try to develop training for others to achieve *best practice*. The aim is to move everyone into the *high performer* bracket.

Continuous training and support quite simply means providing everyone with the capability and opportunity of constantly assessing their own performance against agreed standards, and then taking action to undertake the learning that they think will help them to improve. It is critical to avoiding human obsolescence and to giving individuals a real part in determining their own futures.

Key points

- Little if any effective training takes place on the job, though a good deal of learning is done.
- What is needed is some means whereby individuals can receive continuous updating and training, when they need it, when they ask for it, and delivered to them in their workplace. This can be provided by supervisors, more experienced colleagues, or via the technology they use in their daily work.
- Continuous training is a three-stage process of learning, practising, and reviewing performance.
- The review must tell people three things;
  —how they are performing—preferably in relation to some predetermined and measurable standard;
  —why they are performing at that level; and
  —what action they can take to improve.
- There are three groups involved in establishing the criteria and standards for measuring performance:
  —the individuals being measured;
  —their supervisors; and
  —their manager.
- Trainers have different ideas about what coaching is. It might be useful if I offer a definition:
  Motivating, encouraging and helping an individual to improve performance.

15 Learning environments

People learn best in environments directly related to the learning that is taking place, and ones that are planned to cater specifically for the needs of the learning group. There are three main environments in which people learn and grow: the living environment; the working environment; and the education and training environment.

The living environment

People spend a large proportion of their time in the living environment. This is an environment in which everyone learns a great deal, little of which is directly related to the work they do. This environment is ideally suited to learning. It is constantly challenging, and people have to learn to live with themselves and others, and to develop a wide range of social skills, none of which are learnt in a formal way. In fact most people probably don't realize that they are learning. By living, people are learning and growing every day. New experiences are constantly sought out, or faced unexpectedly, and handled with varying degrees of success. People take risks and gradually learn, mostly from experience, how to live a socially responsible life.

The extent of the learning people do in this environment is probably greater than in any other. Little of what people learn about life is taught, and only a small amount is gained from intentional learning activities, and yet everyone learns and grows. If people were not naturally equipped to learn in this way they would not survive. The ability to learn is one of of the most important natural and inherent abilities that people have. The new-born child is learning from the very moment of birth, and research suggests they may even be learning while in the womb.

The working environment

In this environment, as in all others, people learn most about what they do by actually doing it. People learn from their superiors, and from their colleagues. This learning is intentional, in that people ask about the things they need to do, and how to do them, but yet it is not done as a specific learning activity, it is done in the course of doing the job.

This natural learning while doing the job is not what I mean by 'on the job' training. This natural learning is the result of people using their inherent learning abilities to enquire, to observe, to copy, to experiment, and to explore the environment in which they work. It is the same process that everyone uses in the living environment, and is just as effective.

The old apprenticeship approach which has served society for thousands of years used this natural ability. By placing a learner with a master the learner gradually acquired the master's skills. This happened even if the masters made no real effort to teach their apprentices. The process took many years, and the skills of the apprentices rarely exceeded the skills of their masters, hence the better masters were able to charge a higher fee for taking on an apprentice.

In some cultures this approach is still followed with skills being passed from parent to child, and being kept in the family. In the developed world this apprenticeship system has fallen out of favour. The main reason for this is the rapidly changing world in which people live and work. Skills which were of value a few years ago are now obsolete. The learning process has also been speeded up with the use of specific and intensive training schemes. However, many people believe that this is a move in the wrong direction and that the apprenticeship system should be retained and expanded.

In spite of these changes people still learn the greater part of what they know and can do, and develop their attitudes and behaviour from actually doing things, i.e. working. All around them there are examples of what to do, how to do it. and how to think about it. The power of the working environment can and often does outweigh any training that might take place. This works in both a positive and a negative way. Good working environments develop skilled people with appropriate attitudes and behaviour; poor working environments do the exact opposite.

It is difficult if not impossible to train people to work in a way that does not fit neatly into their working environment. Because of this it is vital that the working environment reflects all the values of the learning organization.

The education and training environment

The education and training environment is one in which an opportunity is created for people to acquire knowledge, skills and attitudes, and to change behaviour in some predetermined way. Situations are set up in which people have the opportunity to learn specific things. For most people the first experience of this kind of environment is school.

School is a part of life, and yet it is a specific well-defined opportunity to learn. What is to be learned and how it is to be learned is well established, and people are specially trained to enable the learning to take place. Teaching is a highly skilled job which all too often is frustrated because the learners do not see the sense and relevance in what they are being asked to learn. What is being taught in schools frequently bears no relationship to the reality of the lives the students are living.

Many people see their time at school as a struggle to learn what other people wanted them to learn so that they could pass an examination. Because society then judges them on the results of those examinations the whole process becomes one of extreme pressure and stress, hardly conducive to effective learning.

School is followed by college, and possibly university where the same attitudes to learning and teaching continue. Though there is more choice for the student they are still taught and given masses of information which is used once again to pass examinations. Once they have passed the dreaded examination hurdle (I have yet to meet anyone who enjoys exams) many people simply press the delete button and remove most of the information they have remembered from their cluttered brains. By the time students enter the workforce they are conditioned to expect to be taught all they need to know, and many people have simply had their inherent learning skills shut down. Rediscovering learning power in relation to work is a major adjustment that many people have to make. Training is used to help this process, but unfortunately much training follows the 'information giving' approach of college and university. People find this comfortable, but they don't learn well, and when they return to the workplace their training is overtaken by the experiences of work.

It is perfectly feasible to provide learners with information, either by presenting it to them in the usual 'talk and chalk' way, or by guiding them to suitable sources where they can obtain it. It is also useful from time to time to direct the learning process along the most suitable path. But when doing this it is important to ensure that the learning is closely related to working activities. Training that relates closely to the working environment does help to move people forward, but this training has to be carefully designed to fit the learning needs of individuals, and to lead to the performance required by the organization.

This form of learning-centred training can be done 'on the job', or 'off the job', and though I have already said that this differentiation offends me, I have to admit that it is a useful way of distinguishing these two training environments.

On the job training

This is the process by which trainers and managers attempt to provide learning opportunities as an adjunct to the work that is taking place. This may be achieved by learners working with colleagues with the intention of learning (the apprenticeship approach), or alternatively by providing learners with materials and facilities from which they can learn without leaving their workplace.

Within a learning organization managers may arrange work so that staff are faced with new challenging situations from which they can learn or they may receive coaching from their superiors, or have special training meetings and discussions. All of these approaches create the opportunity for people to learn, and should enhance the learning process if they are done effectively. Just leaving people to find their own way may be on the job learning, but it is not on the job training.

Off the job training

Creating off the job learning environments is perhaps the most difficult, yet probably the most widely used approach to training. It is difficult because it removes people from the reality of living and working into an artificial and synthetic environment of which modern training centres are the epitome. In design layout and facilities they usually fall somewhere between a school and a hotel. The rooms frequently look like modern well-equipped classrooms, and the atmosphere is usually ordered, if not regimented. People are expected to fit into this physical environment in order to learn the prescribed things.

Such environments can of course be used in wide variety of ways, but the most common approach is the 'classroom' style, with lecturers standing at the front 'delivering' training to the assembled and neatly arranged learners. Even though it is well known that for many people this is the worst way to learn, many trainers still persist with this approach. If it is done well it can work and people will learn, but it should be closely related to working reality, and be practical.

Even when the training is more experiential it follows a regular pattern of here is some information, now here is a problem, now go into syndicate groups (usually in separate small rooms), deal with the problem, then report back to the main group. There is an immediate sense of competition with the other groups, and often people are more concerned with 'getting it right' than with learning.

In this kind of environment the 'teacher' is often seen as the enemy, someone to be bettered, but certainly not seen as a member of the learning group. Many people faced with this type of learning environment revert to school-like behaviour, almost defying the teacher to teach them. In addition the group of learners tends to have to learn at the 'teacher's' pace, and learn what the 'teacher' thinks they should learn. It is not surprising that people revert to school-like behaviour: they have been put into an environment which virtually replicates the worst aspects of formal education.

Though this form of training environment is common, it is not an effective learning environment. Oh, people learn, but then people can learn in the most difficult circumstances if they want to. However, many people learn little of value from this form of training, and little change takes place when they return to the working environment. Contrast this with the following description of a successful learning environment.

The learning environment was created for a group of senior trainers to learn how to create learning-centred training opportunities. The training was planned as a four-day residential workshop in a modern training centre in Australia. The harsh clinical environment was softened by the wonderful location of the centre; however, inside the centre offered the 'traditional' approach to training. I was working with a co-facilitator from the company, whom I had previously trained. We selected to work the first evening, i.e. the evening prior to the first day of the workshop in the library, in which I placed a circle of chairs. The library was a warm inviting room. We did not use name labels, as I believe these create a barrier to getting to know people, and stop people from asking each other one of the most basic of human questions which is, 'hello I'm Trevor who are you?'.

When we were all together I welcomed everyone and we introduced ourselves. There were twelve in the group so names were soon learned. I then suggested that we had a few decisions to make about where we worked, and how we were to work as a group. At this stage I made it clear that I considered myself a member of the group, and that I hoped to learn a great deal over the next four days.

The group then decided where and how they wanted to work. They chose the large training room we had been allocated, but rejected the classroom style U-shaped arrangement in favour of a circle of comfortable chairs at the other end of the 'classroom', i.e. away from the screens and whiteboards. We settled down in the circle and spent some time looking at what we had come to learn; we each prepared a list of our personal learning objectives, after which we set an agenda for the workshop.

At this point several people asked for a copy of the workshop programme, and felt distinctly uneasy not to have a specific timetable. I explained that I did have an outline plan for the workshop, but that I was keen to see what they wanted to learn rather than to tell them what I thought they should learn. Of course as a member of the group I could contribute to the agenda.

Once we had established an agenda we adjourned for the evening. The following morning I checked through the agenda and asked the group how they wanted to go about learning what was on it. They decided to prioritize the agenda and to start with a group exercise defining the learning-centred approach to training. The workshop continued in this way with the group making decisions about what they wanted to do and how they wanted to do it. My task as the facilitator was to help them to make happen what they wanted to happen.

People in twos, threes, or fours were able to work wherever they wanted, and to get whatever help and information they wanted from the facilitators. They were clearly responsible for their own learning, and they had the freedom to choose how and what they wanted to learn. This is the essence of the learning-centred approach and so the environment mirrored what they were learning.

Quite naturally there was some resistance to the approach. Some people wanted to be 'told' things, and some preferred to sit in a classroom than work in groups. This is not surprising after many years of conditioning to this particular way of learning. However, these people soon settled into the approach. The overall result was excellent, and when at the end of the workshop we checked back to see if we had all achieved our personal learning objectives everyone was fully satisfied. This review included me and my co-facilitator. During the workshop we had joined groups in whatever exercise we were doing so that we were equal members of the learning group. Not only did we all learn, but we had a lot of fun doing so.

This is only one example of a learning-centred learning environment, and there are many ways in which training environments can be adapted to suit the learning that needs to take place. The traditional classroom approach is a long way from the living and working environment of most people, so it is difficult to create an appropriate context in which the learning can take place. Trainers need to look carefully at the outcomes they wish to help the learners achieve, and then devise an environment that is as close to this as it is possible to be.

A really well designed training centre would offer a flexible arrangement of rooms which could be used as offices, as a factory, as the branch of a bank, or whatever else needs to be created. This might include classrooms if teachers are being trained. The key word is flexibility in both layout and equipment, with much if not all of the equipment being mobile. Similarly, lighting should offer a wide range of choices from brightly-lit offices, to softly-lit lounge and dining areas, with every room having these choices. All rooms should have plenty of plants, and drapes to soften the environment. Chairs should be comfortable, and able to cope with working, resting, and lounging. It is also a big help if continuous facilities are available for coffee, tea, and herbal drinks so that people can get a drink whenever they wish.

Breaks should be taken when the learners want one, and lunch and dinner breaks should be moved to fit in with the work taking place. Facilities should be available for playing music as a gentle relaxing background (to be used when appropriate, of course).

So, as can be seen, creating off the job learning environments is both involved and difficult, and requires a great deal of thinking and planning. Perhaps if a really effective learning organization could be created then the need for 'off the job' events would be considerably reduced. However, there will always be times when particular groups of people can benefit from spending time together that wouldn't happen unless a situation was created.

Simulating the living and working environments may be necessary, as it is for training pilots, and people working with dangerous equipment, but it is important to realize that these are simulations. The closer learning environments are to the real world the better. Perhaps 'off the job' training environments should only be considered when it is impossible to do it any other way, or when they can be clearly seen to be a distinct aid to the learning process.

Key points

- People learn best in environments that are directly related to the learning that is taking place, and ones that are planned to cater specifically for the needs of the learning group.
- By living, people are learning and growing every day. New experiences are constantly sought out, or faced unexpectedly, and handled with varying degrees of success.
- In the living environment, as in all others, people learn most about what they do by actually doing it.
- It is difficult if not impossible to train people to work in a way that does not fit neatly into their working environment.
- It is vital that the working environment reflects all the values of the learning organization.
- The education and training environment is one in which an opportunity is created for people to acquire knowledge, skills, and attitudes, and to change behaviour in some predetermined way.
- On the job training is the process by which trainers and managers attempt to provide learning opportunities as an adjunct to the work that is taking place.
- The traditional classroom approach is a long way from the living and working environment of most people, so it is difficult to create an appropriate context in which the learning can take place.

PART SIX

High technology in training

16 New training tools

Training for success in an age of high tech has called for the development of a number of new tools. These tools are not being widely used as I write this chapter, but I am convinced that they will play a major part in training in a high tech future.

I am going to describe four new training tools:

- Embedded computer based training (ECBT)
- Concurrent computer based training (CCBT)
- Expert training systems
- Intelligent 'tutors'

Some readers will wonder why there is no mention of interactive video, compact discs, and viewdata. My reason for this is that I want to concentrate on tools that are new and not as yet in wide use, the three just mentioned are all well known and in quite wide use. They certainly add to the variety and capability of presenting training via computers and in leaving them out of this chapter I am in no way diminishing their value to the perceptive and creative trainer.

The high technology workplace presents the trainer with a number of special problems, and as a profession, trainers do not have a good record for really effective training in this area. One of the reasons is the dichotomy between training about the technology, and about its application. The objective is to train the user in the effective use of the system. This requires the development of the knowledge, skills, attitudes and behaviour appropriate to the effective use of the technology. The technology often gets in the way. Trainers are unsure of the technology and if problems occur confidence runs away like water out of a burst pipe. I would pick out two key factors that will lead to success in overcoming the dichotomy:

1 *Do not train about the technology*

The majority of people working in the high technology workplace have little if any interest in the technology itself. They want to know how to *use* it, not what it is and how it works. The right time to tell them is when their curiosity motivates them to find out. This 'need to know' approach is important in keeping training in the workplace easy and simple.

2 *Concentrate on the job application*

If the users' job is to serve the customer, then design the training to improve the way they do this, *using* the technology.

The use of technology is the means to an end, not an end in itself.

Embedded computer based training

Embedded CBT (ECBT) is a term which was coined in the UK in 1981 to describe an approach different to conventional CBT. The difference is that in ECBT the training is built into the application system running on the computer, whereas conventional CBT simply uses the computer as a training tool without any interface with the application system. Since 1981 I have been pioneering the use of ECBT in large computer systems. The role of ECBT is to build a support service into the computer which will give the user all the help and support they need to use the system effectively.

ECBT is intended to be used in areas of learning concerned with using computer systems; it is not appropriate for the development of human relations skills. Helping people to learn to make effective use of the technology they use in their daily work is done by utilizing the same technology as their main training tool.

ECBT uses technology to help people use technology more effectively

ECBT is concerned with feeding the learning process via demonstration, explanation, experimentation, exploration and practice. It then seeks to assess performance, reinforce learning, and support the user. All of these are done in an integrated way using the same technology the individual will use in the workplace.

The concept of ECBT is an integrated approach to providing user support, but it can be separated into four main sections:

- Interactive Help
- Simulation
- Tutorial
- Learning-management

Interactive Help, simulation and tutorial can be considered as the training element. Learning-management covers both the needs of the learner and the trainer, the most important aspect of which is performance improvement.

There is in addition a fifth element which is the human–machine interface. This involves the parts of the computer system that users interact with, including screen design, response messages, and the mode of interaction.

Interactive Help

This element is a part of the application system and provides a wide range of information to the user, all of which is aimed at making the system easier to use and helping the individual to do a better job. Learners learn using a tool that they know will be available when they are working. They learn and work in a protected environment and because of this they work with greater confidence.

A major aspect of using systems well is the response made when mistakes occur. With interactive Help the user receives a three line ACTION message in place of a cryptic error message: this explains what to do to correct the error. If the user wants more information they can request it for the field that is in error. This is not only more useful, but it also reinforces training, and encourages the user.

Simulation Using the application system complete with Help in a controlled environment is an excellent way to learn. A training database is needed, both to protect the application system, and to ensure that suitable data exist for completion of the exercise. The simulation is usually closely linked with a suitable tutorial. In ECBT when users want to practise a transaction they call for training by selecting it on a menu. The system then provides another choice of a tutorial or a practice session. If users select a practice session they are then linked to the part of the system that they want to practise. When the practice is completed a report is produced on the performance levels. Users can then leave the training and return to using the application system.

Tutorial Tutorials which demonstrate, explain and assess knowledge are a desirable precursor to practice. The more demonstrative and interactive the better. Here is an example of a tutorial I have recently been involved with. The system uses a series of screens for entering information about customers who want to open a new account. The tutorial is divided into four parts:

- guided demonstration and explanation;
- controlled walkthrough;
- practice; and
- review.

Learners are taken through the system with data being entered by the training program, and with explanations being given in windows (special areas overlaid) on the operational screen. This is followed by a guided walkthrough with learners entering data on request. The requests appear in windows on the screen. Learners are then given the system to practise with using a printed set of data. Following the practice the work done by learners is reviewed, and the whole training process summarized.

Tutorials do therefore have to link to simulations, calling for them as required. They have to accept learner input and be able to respond to the input. Depending upon the learners' performance they have to be able to offer learners alternative ways to go through the training so that it is effective for each individual. The simulation can also be used to explore the system, and to experiment with ways of doing things.

Learning-management The management element of ECBT must be able to collect data about the learner's activity during the learning process, and if possible during the use of the application system. It is important to be able to collect data which enable users' performance to be assessed, and to maintain files which show performance improvements over time. Monitoring performance before, during and after training is a key factor in offering advice on improving performance.

The primary benefit is undoubtedly improved performance. In ECBT individuals improve their performance through a continuous three-stage process. The three stages are, learning, practising, and reviewing (see Chapter 14). Here is a case study about the application of ECBT.

Westpac Banking Corporation is the 66th largest bank in the world. It is the largest banking group in Australia, and operates in 24 countries. Its global assets total approximately $A84 billion. The bank has over 2000 offices, with a total staff complement in excess of 38 000. Westpac are currently developing a major new computer system to integrate their banking services. The bank uses one of the world's largest IBM computer networks, the centre of which is in Sydney. Computer technology is an important component in the bank's development of efficient high quality services for its customers. Because of its dependence on computer systems Westpac need to ensure its staff are able to use its systems with confidence and efficiency.

As the systems are subject to constant change as new products are introduced, and as improvements are made in procedures, it is necessary for staff to be continuously trained. This places both a time and cost burden on the introduction of new products and new procedures. Westpac Training Services Pty Ltd, a subsidiary of the bank, and one of Australia's largest training companies, were faced with the challenge of finding ways to remove the time and cost burden imposed by system changes.

Why embedded CBT?

In March 1986 a member of Westpac Training's R&D team saw an article on ECBT written by the author of this book. Westpac Training had decided to commission a study into the feasibility and financial justification of ECBT. The investment in time and effort needed to implement ECBT was justified on the basis of the improved use of computer systems, and the reduction in the time and cost involved in implementing new systems.

The proposed plans to re-vamp the bank's systems completely over a five-year period had been approved, and ECBT was added as an important way of ensuring that the new systems were easy to use and easy to learn. It was decided that ECBT would be installed in stages over the life of the systems project, so that on conclusion of the project the full benefits of ECBT would be realized.

The implications of ECBT

The decision to install ECBT had several significant implications. Perhaps the most important of these was the need to rethink the approach to screen design and the way that information would be presented to system users by the system. The next implication was the need to involve training staff in the system design stage, and for training to take over the responsibility for the design and writing of all messages presented to the users by the system.

The third implication was the need for the system architecture to be developed to enable the ECBT system to use the live application system to construct appropriate simulations for use in training sessions.

The fourth implication was the need to find a way of producing training tutorials which could be held on the mainframe, and downloaded to workstations when required. These tutorials had to be able to call for parts of the application system, and monitor and record what was happening during the tutorial.

The fifth implication was for the system to be able to monitor the operational activity of users so that performance could be monitored, and suggestions made for training.

Each of these implications has been addressed, and if not yet fully implemented plans have been agreed for dealing with them.

The majority of people working in the high technology workplace have little if any interest in the technology itself. They want to know how to use it, *not* what it is and how it works. This 'need to know' approach is important in keeping training in the workplace easy and simple.

To get a sense of how ECBT works here is a brief scenario:

> The new system user is shown how to switch on and log-on by the supervisor.
>
> The ECBT system provides an introductory tutorial, which gets the learner to respond; the response is important to avoid a passive attitude.
>
> The system moves on to a tutorial containing a demonstration of how to use the application system using a section of the live system in a controlled simulation, with some response from the learner.
>
> On completion the learner is asked a few questions. Depending upon the answers the system does one of the following,
>
> - moves on
> - returns to the previous tutorial
> - branches to a different, simpler, longer tutorial
>
> The ECBT system now presents learners with a message on how they are doing and offers them an exercise giving a choice of:
>
> - elementary
> - basic
> - advanced
>
> The exercise is a simulation using the live system supported by help and additional printed materials if necessary.
>
> The learner carries out the exercise.
>
> The ECBT system records activity, time, errors, etc. and presents a review to the learner. The learner is asked to respond with information about the training, and is then guided through the sign-off.

The four main elements of ECBT can be seen at work in the scenario. They are: help, simulation, tutorial, and learning-management.

Progress to date

The progress at Westpac has been excellent. In an eighteen-month period a complete ECBT team have been recruited and trained; a methodology for developing ECBT has been written and implemented; the interface between training and systems has been established, and is working well; the procedures for writing Help and creating the Help data base have been put in place; the Help part of ECBT is up and running; tutorials are being built; and the simulation facility is almost complete.

The ECBT package when complete will consist of the following, linked in an integrated way:

- live application system, with an improved user interface
- contextual help (messages in relation to the way the system is being used)
- training data base
- tutorial system
- supporting materials
- performance monitoring
- training management data base
- performance improvement

The performance improvement element will be, of necessity, the final element to be introduced, but this will not prevent the benefits from being realized. Even Help on its own can make systems much easier to use, and therefore less training needs to be carried out. It is anticipated that ECBT will reduce systems training significantly, and also reduce the time and cost of producing user guides and manuals that are no longer needed.

The benefits

Westpac anticipate significant benefits from building ECBT into their CS90 system:

- Improved performance, bringing increased profits via improved accuracy, increased productivity and improved sales and service.
- Reduced training costs, and increased training effectiveness. By reducing the need for training, and by doing the training that is needed in a better way, substantial savings are expected.
- A competitive edge, by improving people's performance, particularly in the way that they use the technology in which the bank has invested a great deal.

Embedded CBT and the future

As ECBT becomes better established at Westpac it will be possible to consider using expert systems to increase the relevance and interactivity of the responses given to users. It will in addition be possible to consider the design and building of systems which are self-explanatory and, therefore, very easy to use. This will lead to the development of systems that are error free, and for which training is simply unnecessary. Removing the need for producing manuals, and the need to train users, will considerably speed up the introduction of new products and procedures, as well as reducing system implementation timescales and costs.

Westpac see ECBT as a visionary way to move into the high technology future that awaits us all. The progress so far indicates that this vision is well on its way to becoming a reality.

The case study quoted above describes the first elements of what will become a comprehensive performance support system (see Chapter 19).

Concurrent computer based training

When a system has already been developed it is not possible to redesign the user interface. Nor is it possible to include within the system the key elements of a continuous training and support system as can be done with ECBT. It is possible however to add information to the system using concurrent CBT.

Concurrent CBT is a new technology which makes it easy for a computer user to learn how to use a computer package, or in-house system. Whether the system is a spreadsheet, a word processing package, or a company's own mainframe system, the first-time user has a lot of problems learning how to use all its functions and features. Unless of course the system incorporates ECBT.

Traditional methods used in training, i.e. courses, tutorials and manuals, are not ideal. The trainer has to learn and remember everything; there is not enough time to practice, and Help support and explanation is inadequate.

The best way remains for learners to have their own personal expert seated next to them guiding them through the use of the system, especially when much of the language is in computer jargon. This expert is ready to help them avoid making mistakes, and to explain what went wrong when it inevitably does! But how can such an expert be made available to every computer user who doesn't have ECBT? The answer is concurrent CBT.

Concurrent CBT operates 'concurrently' with a working computer system, either a package such as Lotus 123, or a mainframe system. By pressing a key the learner calls a training window onto the screen. Training windows contain explanations and advice that guide learners through the steps of a task controlling the 'real' system as it goes. At any time learners can switch the windows off and apply what they have learned. But it is after training that concurrent technology really comes into its own.

Information to help people use the system should be in one place and one place only. In the computer! Following training, new inexperienced users have the problem of 'what do I do next', 'why isn't it doing what I thought it should?' To have to rush off and consult a manual or ring a 'hot line' are neither efficient nor satisfactory ways of solving the problem. With ECBT such information is built into the system and is always available.

Concurrent technology enables a trainer to build help and support material onto the computer itself to run alongside the operating system. This help and support lies dormant while users are operating the system satisfactorily. However, as soon as they encounter a difficulty the pressing of a designated 'hot key' brings up the help and support information immediately. It overlays the screen being used at that moment without in any way affecting the applications sequence of working or data being entered. When the problem has been diagnosed and solved users hit the ESC (Escape) key and carry on where they left off.

When concurrent CBT has been installed the use of the application system is controlled by the training programme even though learners are actually using the 'real' application system. The work learners do during training is 'filtered' by the CCBT to ensure that the training exercise designed by the trainer is completed, and what was required to be learned is learned. The CCBT can also monitor what has happened and provide feedback on the learner's performance.

CCBT is practical and flexible, and there are several pieces of software that can be used to produce it. It has to run on a PC, and though it interfaces with the live system, it is not as comprehensive or as integrated as ECBT, particularly when a mainframe network is involved.

Expert systems

Expert systems consist of three elements:

- A knowledge base
- A set of rules on how to use the knowledge base (which is called an inference engine)
- An interface with the real world

The potential of expert systems for the trainer lies in the ability to manipulate large amounts of information held in the knowledge base, and to explain (reasoning on the basis of the rule set) why the information leads to the stated conclusions. Learners can be presented with a variety of problems for which information has to be accessed and used to arrive at a solution. The expert system can watch this process and then indicate, with reasons, why certain information led to certain results, and how other information would have led to different, possibly better, results.

This could be very powerful when dealing with learning in areas such as diagnosis, evaluation, choice of best approach, and decision making. This is made even more effective if the expert system has been built specifically for the subject domain that the learners are working in.

Expert systems shells (an empty system, a framework on which to hang information) exist, which allow the knowledge base to be populated and the rule set constructed, thus allowing trainers to build their own expert training tools. This does, however, require skills in logic design, and in the programming of the rule sets.

Expert systems can also impact on training when they are used to support people who, in the past, would have needed to learn a great deal of information about the job they are doing. This can now be stored in the knowledge base, and accessed in an expert way. This is done using the inference engine (a set of rules) built by 'experts' in the field. The effect is to remove the need for the original learning to take place. This creates a dependency on expert systems which, for some people, might not be acceptable.

Here is an example of an expert system developed to help trainers produce CBT for computer systems.

An innovative Israeli software company has produced a system that automatically creates a CBT tutorial and exercises, from the minimum of data about the target system. This piece of software is called ACE (Automated Courseware Expert). I have recently completed an intensive review of ACE, including building a short CBT programme for a Lotus 123 application, and facilitating the learning of a new group of users.

The ACE system can best be described as a CBT-automated production tool. It is an 'expert' system which manages a series of knowledge bases in accordance with a range of 'rule sets' (there are over 800 in the current version). The system has been developed to receive a set of information about a computer-based system, and from this information to create a computer based training programme.

The system is aimed specifically at producing training for computer applications. It is not considered by its developers to be appropriate for producing CBT that is of a more generic nature, although with some imagination this seems perfectly feasible to me.

ACE is a menu-based system that runs on a DEC Microvax 3. It uses windows for the menus, and a mouse for selecting the desired option, although there is, of course, a keyboard for entering text. The extensive use of windows sometimes leads to having many windows on the screen at the same time: I counted eight in one example.

ACE uses the information it is given to produce CBT courses according to rule sets. These are used by ACE in accordance with design parameters selected during the specification phase. The layout of screens, the use of text, creation of exercises and tests, are all determined by the system in accordance with the selected design parameters.

There is no doubt that ACE can remove a considerable amount of work from producing CBT courses, especially the drudgery of programming using an authoring system. Once produced, the courses are very easy to maintain. A simple change to any aspect of the subject system could mean far-reaching changes to the course. With ACE the change is entered and ACE does the rest, producing a completely revised course in minutes.

ACE has not been designed to produce either embedded CBT or concurrent CBT. The design philosophy has been to concentrate on producing stand-alone PC-based CBT courses for 'existing' computer applications, running separately from the application itself. However, the ability of ACE to capture the target system, and replicate it exactly as it appears in the live system, is a major advantage for the learner.

ACE lends itself to developing CBT courses alongside systems development, using a prototyping approach (building a representative model of a sequence of screens). If it is unable to capture a screen from the system because that part of the system doesn't yet exist, it can copy a paper-based version of the screen using an optical scanner. It can in addition copy forms and pictures using single frames of video via a PC, and lets the user design a picture with ACE's own graphics editor.

Apart from the extensive rule base ACE incorporates a natural language processor that 'writes' sentence as appropriate for the sense of the text to support the learning. When I entered the statement 'create a graph' as the title of a lesson ACE was able to produce sentences such as, 'you have just created a graph', and 'creating a graph requires you to', and so on. This takes some getting used to. Even with such capabilities it is unlikely that ACE will produce exactly the lesson that you want, so, during the design phase, there is an extensive and simple process for editing the CBT programme. When you are happy with the finished product, or even before if you are in a hurry and not bothered about quality, you can produce the programme on a floppy disk ready for use on an IBM PC or compatible.

The estimated time taken to produce a good quality CBT programme is about 40 hours for one hour of CBT, an estimate I can verify from the work that I did. This compares with anything between 200 and 300 to one for producing CBT. But this is not the only productivity gain. When changes take place, as they frequently do with computer systems, the ACE-produced CBT programme can be amended and re-produced in a few hours, simply by amending the original data on the database and automatically producing a new version.

Some CBT authors might consider the output of ACE to be lacking in colours and flashy graphics, but this need not be the case. One of the obvious limits is that when a system is captured ACE replicates the colours of the captured system, which could be monochrome. This is good for the learner who sees the target system exactly as they will see it in the live system.

ACE is one of the most exciting developments I have seen and worked with in the application of computer technology to training. I am sure that it is going to become standard equipment for the training department of those organizations where the use of technology is critical to success. At last we have the means of delivering effective computer based training into the workplace, of a quality, and at a cost, that only a short time ago would have seemed impossible.

The use of expert systems as supporting systems for computer users will have the effect of considerably reducing the training needed for certain tasks. An example of this is a system that provides bankers with a means of assessing the suitability of a applicant for a loan.

The expert system has been developed and built with the help of very experienced lending executives who have indicated the information needed and its implications for the lending decision.

New lenders use the system which asks them for information before coming up with suggestions for action. At any time lenders can ask the system why it wants the information, or how it has arrived at its suggestions. The system gives its reasons for what it is doing. Such systems will reduce the training needed for new lending executives, particularly in respect to the criteria being used for assessment.

Expert systems are still in an early stage of development, but there are more and more examples of their being used in an effective and practical way. Trainers should invest some time and effort in looking at the possibilities that expert systems present.

Intelligent 'tutors'

Creating a computer based training programme that can be managed by an 'intelligent tutor' is a potentially exciting prospect. Instead of the traditional 'page turning' CBT with so-called interaction with the learner a really meaningful dialogue can be developed. What is required is a computer-based tutorial linked to an expert system, which is able to monitor the learning interaction that is taking place. As the 'tutor' picks up information from the learner's responses it is able to direct the tutorial to present more relevant information, or to return and review information. If the learner wants to find out what is happening the 'tutor' will explain its reasoning.

For this approach to work, every CBT programme will need to have a specific 'tutor' attached. It might be possible to design and build a 'tutor' shell, which will need to be populated with the specific knowledge and rules for the subject being dealt with, together with rules for learning intervention. The biggest problem will be deciding the appropriate points for learning intervention, and this will mean that effective 'intelligent tutors' are only going to be built by people with an extensive knowledge of, and skill in applying, learning psychology.

The development of 'intelligent tutors' is currently an area of research being pursued by a number of universities and companies interested in expert systems and artificial intelligence. The outcomes of this research will need to be carefully examined to determine whether the application of 'intelligent tutors' is going to be practical and have the effect of improving learning.

Conclusion

In this chapter I have looked at four new training tools that are available, or becoming available. All of these tools depend on technology; they do not necessarily replace conventional training, but together with CBT, interactive video, compact disc, and viewdata, they form a vast array of tools to support the performance of people at work.

If trainers are committed to the process of 'helping people to learn', then they have to be informed and skilled enough, as trainers, to use all the approaches available to give learners the best possible learning opportunities.

Key points

- The majority of people working in the high technology workplace have little if any interest in the technology itself. They want to know how to *use* it, not what it is and how it works.
- The role of ECBT is to build a support service into the computer that will give the user all the help and support they need to use the system effectively.
- ECBT is concerned with feeding the learning process via demonstration, explanation, experimentation, exploration, and practice. It then seeks to assess performance, reinforce learning, and support the user. All of these are done in an integrated way using the same technology that the individual will use in the workplace.
- When a system has already been developed it is not possible to redesign the user interface. Nor is it possible to include within the system the key elements of a continuous training and support system as can be done with ECBT. It is possible however to add information to the system using concurrent CBT.
- Expert systems consist of three elements:
  —A knowledge base.
  —A set of rules on how to use the knowledge base (which is called an inference engine).
  —An interface with the real world.
- Creating a computer based training programme that can be managed by an 'intelligent tutor' is a potentially exciting prospect. Instead of the traditional 'page turning' CBT with so-called interaction with the learner, a really meaningful dialogue can be developed.

17 Computer screen standards

Objective

In ECBT, CCBT and other more conventional forms of CBT, training material is presented to learners via a computer screen. The purpose of this standard is intended to set out the best way to do this. There are three key aims:

- To establish the preferred screen layout for presenting training material.
- To explain the key aspects of reading material from a screen.
- To set guidelines for dealing with learner interaction.

The approach: guidelines

This standard is aimed at training analysts who have to write materials that are to be presented to learners via the screen. This may have to be carried out within the constraints established by the systems people for screen layout. This standard should be read in the context of any existing screen design standards.

The computer screen enables information to be presented with a considerable amount of flexibility. It can also provide the opportunity of using a wide range of colours. The factors that control the presentation of training material through this medium are:

- screen size and layout
- colours
- windowing
- data insertion
- interaction

The standard deals with each of these factors in turn and provides recommended ways of dealing with each in the context of presenting training material. The decision as to whether material is best presented via the computer screen or in a printed format rests, of course, with the designer; however, this standard may affect the choice of approach.

The approach: standards

One of the aims of any standard is to ensure that consistency of approach is maintained. This is particularly relevant in the case of presenting training material via a computer screen. Learners will soon get used to the way information is presented, and will expect this to continue. Some organizations have had considerable difficultly in using CBT packages produced by different companies using varying standards.

The use of computers in training means that learners' memories do not need to be burdened with detailed information during the training. This helps the learning process. If ECBT is being used then the need for learning a great deal of data is removed. It should not be necessary for learners to be referred to their own memories, as in the statement '. . . as you will remember', or '. . . as you will recall'.

People who are learning need all their faculties to remember what is going on at the present time. Cluttering their memories with data that could easily be referred to on screen, makes the learning process more difficult.

Screen size and layout

The standard computer screen size is expressed in terms of so many lines of text, and so many characters per line. The normal size is, 24 lines of 80 characters. It is wise to check the screen size of the computer on which the training is to be based, and also to check the availability of lines and characters, as it is usual for a certain amount of space to be taken up by program codes.

The layout of training screens should follow the basic approach used in printed material, i.e. left to right, and top to bottom. This means that information should be presented on the screen in its natural logical sequence starting at the top left-hand corner and finishing at the bottom right-hand corner.

The way that text is set out on the screen should enable learners to recognize quickly and easily where they are. This means that the information should be laid out as it would be on a page of printed text, using headings, highlighting, spacing, and varying text.

Headings

Headings to sections of text should be in capitals. Sub-headings within sections should be in upper and lower case underlined.

Highlighting

The facilities on most computers for highlighting sections of text makes this a tempting feature to use. It can, however, be very confusing to learners. The main highlighting features and their recommended use are indicated below:

- reverse video   for fields where data has to be input.
- underlining   for sub-headings.
- flashing   for fields in error.
- bold or bright   for emphasis of important points.

If other highlighting features are available then the temptation to use them should be resisted.

Spacing

One line should be left blank between a heading and the text, and one line between the text and the next heading or sub-heading. One character space should be left between the edge of the screen and the text, on both the left- and right-hand margins.

Space is usually at a premium on computer screens, but this is no excuse for producing badly set out and cramped information.

Varying text On many computers it is possible to vary the size and type style of text. There are only two instances when this should be done:

- increase the size for headings
- use italic for examples and quotations

Any additional features that are available should be ignored.

Colours The modern computer, especially the PC, can have a considerable array of colours to chose from. Many people get carried away with this splendid opportunity to indulge their artistic fancy. The result is, usually, horrific combinations of colours that, far from enhancing the material, are a definite distraction.

Only six colours should be used:

- black
- red
- white
- green
- yellow
- blue

The purpose in using colours is to provide interest and contrast. The contrast that is provided should be a soft contrast, where the eye has no problem in differentiating the colours, and hence the information from the background. The recommended colour combinations are shown below, the first column being the information and the second being the background.

Information	*on*	*Background*
White	on	Black
Black	on	White
White	on	Blue
Yellow	on	Blue
Red	on	White
White	on	Green
Green	on	White
Blue	on	White

When using colour, designers should be careful to ensure that they do not introduce conflicting colours, e.g. if there is a black screen with white information, and a window is to be introduced, the background of the window could be blue, with white or yellow information. Either way only four colours have been used in total. The maximum should be five, when one is either black or white.

Windowing A window is a section of the screen which is used to overlay the background screen with additional information. The window can be programmed to appear in any part of the screen that is specified. The technique is widely used in PC software, and is a feature of some training software. This standard deals with positioning, borders, and text.

Positioning The window should be positioned as near to the top left-hand corner of the screen as is possible, without obscuring the text, to which it refers, on the background screen. When a second window is displayed, it should not obscure the first window, and it should be positioned so that its top left-hand corner is as near as possible to the bottom right-hand corner of the first window.

A maximum of two windows should be displayed at the same time.

Where a window refers directly to a particular field on the background screen, its top left-hand corner should be as close as possible to the field, and/or should be linked, with an arrow.

Borders Borders to windows should be either a single or a double line, and in the same colour as the information in the window.

Text When text in the window covers both information and instruction to the learner, the instruction should be in a separate section of the window, divided by a single line of the same colour as the border.

The layout of text within a window should follow the same standard as the general screen layout.

Data insertion

The training material that is being produced may require learners to input some information. This must be carefully controlled, or the advantage of learners' participation will be lost. It is important when thinking about data input to follow three standards, concerning:

- instruction
- data availability
- error management

Instruction Learners should be asked for the data that are required, and should be instructed how and where they should be input.

Data availability When learners are asked to input data it should be provided, either as part of the instruction, e.g. *input the customer name as George Derby*, or by reference to a specific page of a training guide. In either case it is possible for the designer to ensure that the training programme knows what to expect, and can respond accordingly.

Error management There are three aspects to error management during training:

- prevention
- cause
- correction

The objective is either to prevent learners from making mistakes, or to explain the reason for mistakes, and provide guidance as to how to overcome the problem.

Prevention This is achieved by preventing learners from inputting the wrong data. Unless exactly the right data is keyed in the system should bleep, and wait for the correct data.

Cause If learners input the wrong data the system should recognize it, and report back to them, giving the reason why the problem has occurred.

Correction If an error does occur, the program should explain how to correct the error, and enable learners to do so.

Interaction

When learners are asked to interact with the training programme, whether it is to input data, or to answer a question, the programme should provide enough information to enable them to interact effectively. This will cover four factors:

- action
- feedback
- undos
- responses

Action The action that learners have to take to operate the training programme should be simple and consistent. The following are the main standards:

Enter key— when data have been input which the programme needs to react to.

Space bar— to move the programme forward to the next screen of information.

Escape key— to return to the menu, or the start of the segment of the programme being worked on.

Feedback This is the process of replying to learners in respect of the interaction that has taken place. Every time there is some action on the part of the learner, there should be some appropriate reaction (feedback) from the training programme.

Undos There is nothing worse, when learning, than to be unable to undo some action which is known to be wrong, and to have to wait for the programme to report an error. It should always be possible to escape to the beginning.

It is essential that the programme provides, wherever possible, the facility for learners to undo what they have already done. This can be achieved by repeating what they have done and asking them to confirm that it is what they want to do, before proceeding.

Responses All responses that the programme makes to any action of learners, should be,

- affirmative,
- non-patronizing,
- reinforcing,
- in the second person,
- encouraging, and
- lead on naturally, and logically to the next point.

Conclusion

The presentation of information via a computer screen is the primary element of the user interface. If care and attention is paid to keeping the information simple and supportive, users will be able to learn and use systems with ease. These standards are a first step in this process. Trainers should use all the pressure they can to persuade system designers to follow them.

Key points

- One of the aims of any standard is to ensure that consistency of approach is maintained. This is particularly relevant in the case of presenting training material via a computer screen.
- People who are learning need all their faculties to remember what is going on. Cluttering their memories with data that can easily be referred to on screen, makes the learning process more difficult.
- Space is usually at a premium on computer screens, but this is no excuse for producing badly set out and cramped information.
- Many people get carried away with the wide range of colours available. The result is, usually, horrific combinations of colours that, far from enhancing the material, are a definite distraction.
- When learners are asked to interact with the training programme, whether it is to input data, or to answer a question, the programme should provide enough information to enable them to interact effectively.
- The action which learners have to take to operate the training programme should be simple and consistent.
- Every time there is some action on the part of the learner, there should be some appropriate reaction (feedback) from the training programme.
- It is essential that the programme provides, wherever possible, the facility for learners to undo what they have already done.

18 Electronic performance support systems

By Gloria J. Gery

In nearly three decades of watching people and organizations develop hardware and software to support human performance, many of us have become inured to technological advances. We expect more power, smaller size, faster performance, and increased intelligence in cheaper packages. Desktop mega storage, high-resolution displays, and image compression algorithms cease to amaze us. Networks, software interfaces, hypermedia, and artificial intelligence are becoming part of our mental furniture. It gets my attention however when someone comes up with new uses for the technology. Without deprecating the magnitude of the achievements in hardware and software of the past several years, I believe that the most significant advances in the improvement of human performance will come, not from the technical achievements, but from the shrewdness with which the technology is applied.

There is a barely emerging concept in the performance and instruction field, one that I consider to be the most exciting development in this business in the past generation. It is not a technical development (although technical developments are making it increasingly feasible); it is an intellectual concept, a perspective on human performance, that promises to change significantly the way that we look at the workplace and how people operate in it. It is the concept of *electronic performance support systems.*

An electronic performance support system is a concept, not a particular technology. Technology stands behind it, but the concept is what is critical. (Note: Although in this chapter I will often be using the term 'performance support system' I mean for the qualifier 'electronic' to be understood. There are other performance support systems, related to reward systems, job design, and organizational structure, which are important, but are beyond the scope of this chapter.)

What do I mean by performance support system? Essentially, an electronic performance support system is an integrated electronic environment that is available to and easily accessible by each employee. It is structured to provide immediate, individualized on-line access to the full range of information, software, guidance, advice and assistance, data, images, tools, and assessment and monitoring systems to permit employees to perform their jobs with a minimum of support and intervention by others.

One part of the performance support system is the data base holding the data a human being needs or will manipulate in doing a job. It can take any form we have come to expect of a data base:

- *Traditional data bases* containing numbers, graphics libraries, and other 'data'.
- *Text data bases* including on-line documentation such as procedures, policy and product information, concepts and explanations, specifications, business policy, glossaries, commands, and so on, as well as stored images of text relevant to the job (memos, reports, etc.).
- *Visual data bases* including libraries of pictures, schematics, diagrams, graphics, maps, and full motion video, to provide information or serve as models, representative images, reference points, and so forth. In these visual data bases, video and images are viewed as a data element—both from a technical and a structural perspective.
- *Audio data bases* with libraries of sounds and words/word sequences, and music in a form that can be heard and understood by people.
- *Information services* such as Dow Jones News Retrieval.

The other part of the system is the help that supports the user in doing the job. It can take the form of:

- *Interactive productivity software* including spreadsheets, text processors, task specific interactive job aids and so on.
- *Applications software* to perform specific job tasks or functions (e.g., claim systems, rating, pricing, or estimating systems, CAD/CAM or CASE systems, management reporting systems).
- *Expert or artificial intelligence systems* for problem structuring, decision support, analysis or diagnosis.
- *Help systems* that are user- or system-initiated, context sensitive and inquiry-based, or intelligent. Help systems can include explanations, demonstrations, advice, and alternatives.
- *Interactive training programmes* that permit self-directed or structured learning experiences, which are task related and flexible. Cognitive programs could be available at user request. Programs can be system- or user-initiated.
- *Assessment systems* that permit evaluation of knowledge or skill either before job task performance or in assessing employee competence.
- *Feedback and monitoring systems* that can inform users about the appropriateness of their actions (e.g. error messages and related instructions) or track user activity to determine whether and when assistance or information is needed.
- *A user interface* that provides user-defined access to the above components in a straightforward and consistent way and that permits the integration of relevant components so that a meaningful and whole context is provided for the user to work in.

As I noted the performance support system is a concept rather than a technology. It is not limited to the components I have listed here. Any other components can be included that, either alone or in combination with the above, are useful to someone trying to learn something or perform a task. What is fundamental to the concept is that these things are available to people working when they need them in the form they need them.

A performance support system will derive its power and its impact from these qualities:

Number of support functions

The more methods of support there are in a performance support system, the greater its potential power. For example, the simple availability of on-line Help from within software improves the probability that users will seek information when they don't know what to do; this should translate into the user doing more and doing it better with the system. Or on-line availability of problem structuring tools such as expert or advisory/coaching systems reduces the need for additional human support and improves individual performance.

Quality, completeness, and relevance of the functions

The more complete the universe of data, information and tools within a given function, the more powerful the system. The quality of these functions also affects system power. If the functions are clear, accurate and relevant to the user, they will be more useful. Any cross referencing or 'linking' of functions must relate to the associations made by the user. For example, a cross-referencing system is less useful if it is too technical or incomplete or does not respond to the ways in which users ask for information.

Quality and degree of internal and external integration

How well and in how many ways the system's functions are interrelated affects the power of the system. Such integration also reduces the time and effort required for people to make use of it. The links can be more or less sophisticated. For example, a menu option offers one level of power for simple access to a glossary of terms, a job procedures listing, or an advisory system. The user can browse or search through the appropriate listing or data base or ask for specific assistance. If the access method is context sensitive to the listing, the performance support system is even more powerful, since it does not depend on the user's knowledge or motivation to make use of the appropriate element. Access ease and speed alone increase use.

The obstacle to successful integration is that it usually has to be performed by an already knowledgeable or proficient person, who cross references information or determines what a user would want in a particular situation. The more proficient the person performing the integration, however, the less likely that person can assume the perspective or mind-set of the inexperienced or uninformed user (e.g. to recall points of confusion). But it is critical that the integration reflect the least experienced user's perspectives and associative mental processes.

Integration can be achieved in various technological ways, most powerfully in a true relational data base structure. Less powerful forms would include software indexing systems (e.g. on-line referencing systems), information structuring tools (e.g. Hypercard), hierarchical data bases, or those implemented through programming languages.

The true relational data base structure permits more powerful and flexible integration, improved individualization by users, relative ease of maintenance, and re-usability of system components among and between performance support systems.

Degrees of intelligence

The more a performance support system has 'intelligent' or analytical functions, the more powerful it will be. For example, the availability of 'expert' or 'knowledge' systems to help inexperienced employees to structure complex tasks such as data gathering, analysis, decision making and diagnostic activity can accelerate performance or permit less experienced or capable people to perform more complex tasks successfully.

The performance support system will be more powerful if it includes an intelligent help system to monitor activity, identify error patterns or sub-optimal task performance, and then communicate its findings to the user. At the high end of this scale, we can imagine an intelligent monitoring system that provides explanations or rationale to the user or routes the user into a simulator for practising task performance.

User interface and access to functions

A consistent easy-to-use system interface and straightforward access to its functions is a major source of power. If a system user must learn and recall new, diverse, inconsistent, or complex commands to access parts of the system, its impact is diminished. It simply won't be used unless there is no alternative. If the interface is consistent with other interfaces in use, is intuitively obvious, and is structured to permit easy browsing and selection among available alternatives, the user will be empowered.

To the extent that the interface only displays available alternatives or 'highlights' available options and to the extent that users do not have to work through a series of elaborate hierarchical menus, the more powerful the system. The Apple Macintosh or Microsoft Windows interfaces are examples of presentation systems or interfaces that provide a consistent and simple access framework for users.

Context sensitivity

We usually think of context sensitivity as the system's ability to present information when the user needs it, that is, in the user's current context. I am suggesting something even broader here, going beyond the context of the situation to the contexts of time, condition, and any other relevant factor.

Imagine pharmaceutical sales reps who need to use medical terms to discuss their company's products with doctors. These people could learn the pronunciation of the terms rapidly if they could access an audio pronunciation directly from, say, a product specification document. A performance support system could go even further to cement word knowledge, word sound, and understanding of the term if it them provided access to a visual data base with photographs of the relevant anatomical part or disease condition. If the sales reps could then enter a simulation in which the variables around the drug use could be manipulated (e.g. a simulator in which insulin level, blood sugar level, and drug level relationships could be explored), the reps would more quickly be able to understand, communicate about, and sell a product. If then an immediate comparison could be made with competitor products, yet another level of performance would be achieved.

The number of forms of information

The more media and forms in which information, concepts, explanations, and images are stored and accessible, the more powerful the system. For example, if I can read about, see, and hear about a concept or procedure and can then manipulate it (e.g. within a simulator, via a formula, or in relationship to specific data) I can understand and perform an operation more quickly.

System levels and qualifiers

The more levels of knowledge and skill a performance support system can accommodate, the more powerful it is. If a user can enter into a system based on specific qualifiers such as current competency level, and then move up or down various levels within the system based on range of knowledge, skill, motivation, and confidence, the system's impact increases over a less accommodating one. As a practical matter, the system should allow those qualifiers to be set in advance by managers, to limit access to confidential information, job classification, job function, and so forth. The organization can then tailor a single system to permit use by multiple user populations, much as access to a corporate data base can be centrally controlled.

Access definition is a matter of individual company or manager policy and philosophy, but the system should have the capability to be configured and reconfigured based on changing individual and organization qualifications.

Overall power of the system

There is an interactive and multiplier effect among and between these variables. The effect is not simply cumulative. There are currently no formulae to apply to determine performance support system power, but it is reasonable to assume that power is a function of the completeness, quality, and characteristics of each component and the integration among and between them.

The imperative

The performance support system viewpoint will see widespread adoption in the foreseeable future because of three basic conditions: the availability of the technology, the explosion of creativity in the use of it, and the inadequacy of training as it is now practised.

Availability of technology

Fast, inexpensive, large memory and networked hardware is available. Not only is technology making performance gains, it is generally more available. High performance permits new types of software and sophisticated user interfaces. Integration of previously independent software functions can now occur. Workstations are replacing PCs as the hardware of choice.

- Large, fast, and inexpensive computer processors, including adequate portable computers, are becoming available. Estimates are that personal computers incorporating the Intel 80486 chip will have the processing power of the IBM 3090 mainframe introduced in 1985.
- Inexpensive devices permitting storage of large amounts of conventional data as well as high quality still and full motion images, audio, and large volumes of text are being introduced. In March 1989 Apple

Computer announced the availability of a 160 megabyte hard drive for the Macintosh II for only $2600.

- Data communications networks are becoming ubiquitous.
- Affordable and usable software development tools, concepts such as hypermedia, expert system shells, on-line reference systems, relational data bases for text, images, and audio data, and image processing software are being announced daily.

Explosion of creativity

We are in a period of explosive creativity and related paradigm shifts as a result of all this technology. Several new mind-sets are emerging that will, if spread, expand the number and commitment of those who must become involved to make performance support systems a reality.

- 'Mass Customization' (a concept described by Stanley Davis in *Future Perfect*, Addison-Wesley, 1987), the ability to have widespread availability of generic information, service, or product accessible by many and infinitely tailored by individuals at minimal cost and in virtually immediate timeframes.
- Expectations of consumers, individual employees, and managers to have their particular needs met while obtaining the economic and logistical benefits of mass production and distribution systems.
- Concepts of 'intelligent workstations' are evolving in which previously independent resources (e.g. documentation, training, software, support, information access, etc.) are now integrated and readily accessible to individuals without the involvement of intermediaries.
- Redefinition of how training can occur once integrated performance support systems are available.
- 'Disintermediation', or the elimination of unnecessary or limited value added intermediaries in a process (e.g. replacing bank tellers with Automatic Teller Machines (ATMs); a more relevant example here would be a shift in responsibility for the structuring of learning sequences from instructional designers to learners).

Inadequacy of current training

There is mounting evidence that training programmes as we conduct them today cannot improve employee performance quickly enough to meet changing business conditions.

- Global competition is increasing; profits are inadequate. Customer expectations and other factors have increased requirements for competence and the rate at which it is achieved.
- The rate of change is accelerating and changes are more complex. Change is also affecting virtually all aspects of most businesses (e.g. products, processes, systems, organization structure, and market changes). Increased organizational flexibility and adaptation skills are required to respond to both the changes themselves and the external competitive pressures that drive them.
- Job complexity is increasing and higher level skills involving analysis, synthesis, and extrapolation of knowledge are required. Simple information recall, limited understanding of concepts, and unquestioning compliance with prescribed procedures is inadequate. We now require true in-depth understanding, critical thinking skills, and the ability of employees to act independently within a range of situations.

- For many reasons we must often place people with less knowledge and experience than we require into jobs.
- The costs and consequences of performance gaps are becoming more visible and unacceptable. These include errors, the cost of errors, and the activity and costs associated with error recovery. Poor services and inadequate quality plus inadequate productivity, delayed results, lost sales, and customer dissatisfaction, lead to lower-than-desired business growth and profits. In addition there are problems with turnover and morale among inadequate performers and those who work with them, and failure to achieve anticipated benefits from new systems, products, and procedures.
- The training audience is increasingly heterogeneous and diverse. And the one-size-fits-all training approach is no longer adequate (if it ever was in the first place).

The electronic performance support system concept represents a change in outlook as well as technique. Although it is now emerging, it is doing so only in fits and starts.

It will never really take hold until two critical conditions are fulfilled: there has to be a critical mass of people who understand the technologies involved and how they can be used; and there have to be sufficient strategies and techniques in place to exploit them.

Right now, when new approaches are being implemented (e.g. on-line information access or interactive training), they are typically being developed in functional vacuums by people with narrow views (e.g. by technical documentation or CBT units). As a result, only components of a performance support system are being constructed without regard for the structure, design, and implementation of an integrated system. There have as yet been few people with the overall vision to step forward and attempt merging the different functions into an integrated performance support system.

What vision there is seems to be stuck at too low an organizational level to mobilize the economic, logistical, and political resources necessary to result in development. Those who are building systems are applying new technology to old models rather than reorientating themselves to the possibilities and alternatives that new technologies permit.

As long as we continue in this way we will likely make gains in efficiency (and thereby garner appropriate rewards), but we will never realize the possibilities that technology promises. Without a whole new viewpoint, our performance problems will be decreased, but never seriously addressed.

Key points

- The most significant advances in the improvement of human performance will come, not from the technical achievements, but from the shrewdness with which the technology is applied.
- An electronic performance support system is a concept not a particular technology. Technology stands behind it, but the concept is what is critical.

- Electronic performance support system is an integrated electronic environment that is available to and easily accessible by each employee. It is structured to provide immediate, individualized on-line access to the full range of information, software, guidance, advice and assistance, data, images, tools, and assessment and monitoring systems to permit employees to perform their jobs with a minimum of support and intervention by others.
- What is fundamental to the concept is that these things are available to people working when they need them in the form they need them.
- The obstacle to successful integration is that it usually has to be performed by an already knowledgeable or proficient person, who cross references information or determines what a user would want in a particular situation. The more proficient the person performing the integration, however, the less likely that person can assume the perspective or mind-set of the inexperienced or uninformed user (e.g. to recall points of confusion). But it is critical that the integration reflect the least experienced user's perspectives and associative mental processes.
- The more a performance support system has 'intelligent' or analytical functions, the more powerful it will be.
- To the extent that the interface only displays available alternatives or 'highlights' available options, and to the extent that users do not have to work through a series of elaborate hierarchical menus, the more powerful the system.
- The performance support system viewpoint will see widespread adoption in the foreseeable future because of three basic conditions: the availability of the technology, the explosion of creativity in the use of it, and the inadequacy of training as it is now practised.
- The training audience is increasingly heterogeneous and diverse. And the one-size-fits-all training approach is no longer adequate (if it ever was in the first place).

19 Performance management systems

Any organization's investment in its people will be wasted unless the corporate needs for human abilities, i.e. the knowledge, skills, attitudes, and behaviour of the people, and the personal development of each individual, are fully understood and managed effectively.

What is needed is a fully integrated system that addresses three things:

- Management's needs for the human abilities necessary to perform the work of the organization.
- The individual's needs for personal growth and development.
- Training management's requirement for identifying and meeting the corporate and individual needs.

In the high tech world of the future the training manager has no excuse for not harnessing the power of the computer to help in the effective management of human resources. It is quite feasible to build an integrated computer system to hold information in data bases on organizational needs, the needs of people, and the training available. Such a system would then be able to link these data bases and provide information about where certain human attributes were needed and available.

The corporate view

The organization wants to obtain, develop and keep the people that it needs to carry out its corporate strategy. These needs are not static. They change constantly in response to a wide variety of factors. The management of change is almost completely associated with the way human beings adapt to cope effectively with the changes that occur. It is necessary, therefore, for the organization to be fully aware of its needs for human abilities, and the impact that future developments will, or might, have on the reservoir of talent.

There are three sets of information that must be constantly maintained so that corporate strategies can take full account of the human factor. These are:

- the jobs that need to be done at the present time, and the human abilities needed to do them to the required performance levels;
- anticipated changes to the job structure, and the impact this will have on the needs for human abilities; and

- the extent of the existing human abilities available within the organization.

With this information it is possible to identify any present and anticipated future mismatch between the corporate needs and the human abilities available. Having identified the gap, because there will almost always be one, the organization can then take the necessary decisions about the approach and the investment needed to bridge the gap.

The result of these decisions will be the *human resource strategy*, and will incorporate recruitment policy and training policy. Human resourse development is concerned with trying to answer two main questions:

- How many people, with what abilities, are needed?
- How can the organization best develop existing people to provide the performance needed now and in the future?

The answers to these questions can only be provided if there is a continuous flow of information about the organization and its people, and the capability of analysing this information in terms of performance.

The personal view

All individuals working in an organization have their own views on the way they wish to grow and develop. Such views may not coincide with the corporate view. In fact they very rarely coincide. Individuals will have a view of their current abilities, the way they wish to see them expand, and the aspirations they wish to achieve. Such an individual view may or may not be known to the organization, quite inappropriate plans could be made, and money wasted pursuing a path that individuals might reject.

It is important, therefore, that both the organization and the individual have access to, and can amend, information concerning the following:

- the individual's knowledge and skill base, whether or not it is pertinent to the current job;
- the individual's aspirations in terms of personal growth and development; and
- the level at which the individual currently performs.

This information is required to assess the degree of training that individuals will need in order to develop the abilities required by the organization, or to achieve their own aspirations. If only the former is considered, and if aspirations are ignored, individuals may eventually leave and find a situation more in line with the achievement of their own desires. The investment that has been made in those individuals will then be lost to the organization. Of course people leave organizations for many reasons, most of which boil down to a dissatisfaction with some aspect of work which doesn't meet their personal desires.

The key elements

There are, therefore, three primary elements in the model:

- the organization's needs for human abilities;

- individual needs for personal growth and development; and
- the training needed to match these two.

The ability to meet corporate and individual needs will require a training resource that can respond to both the organization's and the individual's needs in a cost effective way. This will mean assembling comprehensive training facilities and materials that can be delivered to the people who need them, when they are needed, and at an acceptable cost. These training facilities and materials will need to be designed and built to meet specific knowledge, skill, attitude and behaviour needs. The training facilities and materials will have to be specified in terms of the needs that they meet, and the level to which the individual will acquire the appropriate skills, i.e. develop the desired attributes.

Attribute analysis

The use of the term attribute is, I believe, both appropriate and convenient. An attribute is 'a quality assigned to a person or thing' (*Oxford English Dictionary*). It follows that it is possible to assign the qualities required by jobs, qualities held by people, and qualities enhanced by training.

The organization places demands upon the attributes of the people it employs. Individuals provide the organization with the attributes that they have, and are motivated to give to the organization. Training delivers the means by which people acquire additional attributes, or enhance the ones they already have.

It is necessary for the performance management system to provide an appropriate means of analysing attributes for all three key elements. This is called 'attribute profiling' and involves creating attribute profiles for jobs and people, and assessing training in terms of the attributes it can develop.

A job profile consists of three things:

- *the attributes required to do the job*, in terms of what people must know, what they should be able to do, the attitudes they should have, and the required behaviour.
- *the demand level for each attribute*. For example, this may define whether the knowledge and skill is required at an elementary or advanced level.
- *performance indices, and standards*. These indicate the required performance level for people to achieve to be assessed as competent.
  —The index is the unit of measurement, i.e. success rate.
  —The standard is the achievement level, i.e. 98%.

A personal profile consists of:

- *the attributes held*, i.e. the current knowledge and skill possessed, and attitude and behaviour displayed.
- *the level at which these are held*, i.e. elementary or advanced.

A training profile consists of:

- *the attributes needed to commence the training*, i.e. what is the desired level of knowledge, skill, etc. to start the training.

- *the levels attainable on completion of training,* i.e. the level of knowledge, skill etc. possessed by the individual after the training.

Maximizing people power

To make the very best use of the people in the organization, it seems obvious that there should be the closest possible match between the job profile and the personal profile. This will reduce the training needed and hence the cost. In addition it will allow individuals to aspire to levels of performance appropriate to their personal profiles. In coping with change it also becomes possible to identify the most appropriate people, i.e. those with the nearest profile, to be trained to handle the new situation.

The direction in which training effort and investment should be made can also be determined by analysing where attributes are lacking in key business activities. People power is the only real power that any organization has. The performance of any organization is the sum total of the performance of the individuals working in the organization.

Cost benefit model

People are rewarded financially for providing their abilities to the organization. They use these abilities to perform activities that generate the income the organization receives for its products and services. The organization invests in training to enhance the abilities of the people it employs.

- *All the profits of the organization are produced by the efforts of people.*
- *The people are paid, and provided with the resources they need to do their work.*
- *The organization invests in training in order to improve the performance of its people.*

By quantifying these three factors a cost benefit model can be developed which will direct the organization to where the investment in training will produce the best possible returns. This will allow the best use to be made of training resources.

The cost benefit model will identify the key result areas of the business, and indicate the effect of improved performance on these areas. The next step is to decide how the investment in training can be managed to provide the desired improvement in performance.

Creating the performance management system

The complete performance management system is created in three stages:

- Structured task analysis to develop job profiles
- Personal attribute profiling
- Training resource profiling and delivery

Structured task analysis

Structured task analysis is a well known approach to breaking a job down into its constituent activities and tasks. In the model, I extend this by then stating for each task the attributes required to perform the task to the required performance levels. To complete the picture, performance indices and standards have to be determined. This is perhaps the most difficult aspect of developing job profiles.

Personal attribute profiling

All individuals complete a questionnaire or are interviewed to establish their attribute profile. Once this has been done feedback from actual performance can be fed into the system. This process can take a long time to complete, so a self-assessment approach that makes use of a computer is recommended. This can provide an excellent way to gather the information concerning the current attributes of an individual.

Training resource profiling and delivery

There are two aspects to this stage of the development:

- the training available
- the means of delivering the training

The training available

All training, including internal courses, distance learning, computer-based training, external courses, etc. has to be evaluated in terms of the attributes that can be acquired and the starting point for learners. This provides the base from which the needs of the organization and individuals can be met.

The delivery system

The means by which people and training are brought together, and the effect assessed, is handled by the delivery mechanism. This means maintaining detailed records on what training is being provided to whom, when, and for what reason. On completion of training the information on who has done what and the inferred attribute levels now gained is passed to the personal profile system.

The integrated system

With all three stages complete, the system can be fully integrated with individual training needs being identified by performance monitoring, then being met by training and confirmed by further monitoring. The monitoring is both manual and computer based, depending on how computer technology is used by the organization.

I believe that it is perfectly feasible to build a performance management system on any kind of computer, including a PC. The only limitation is in the size of memory to handle the scale of the system needed by the organization. The three information data bases that are created, for jobs, people, and training, can provide opportunities for:

- matching people to jobs
- matching jobs to people
- analysing corporate needs
- analysing personal needs
- determining training and recruitment policy

Naturally it helps if these data bases are held on a computer rather than manually, both in terms of speed of operation and in managing large scale data resources.

The benefits of developing an integrated performance management system as described here can be considerable, and include:

- improved individual performance, through better training
- improved corporate results, through better performance
- better directed investment in training
- higher quality workforce
- lower staff turnover
- faster reaction to change
- greater opportunities for corporate development
- better response to market opportunities
- sharper competitive edge

The effort is by no means small, but then no great achievement ever came without a considerable investment of human effort.

Key points

- Any organization's investment in its people will be wasted unless the corporate needs for human abilities, i.e. the knowledge, skills, attitudes and behaviour of the people, and the personal development of each individual, are fully understood and managed effectively.
- The management of change is almost completely associated with the way human beings adapt to cope effectively with the changes that occur.
- Human resource development is concerned with trying to answer two main questions:
  —How many people, with what abilities, are needed?
  —How can the organization best develop the people they have to provide the performance needed, now and in the future?
- All individuals working in an organization have their own views on the way they wish to grow and develop. Such views may not coincide with the corporate view. In fact they very rarely coincide.
- There are three primary elements in the model:
  —The organization's needs for human abilities;
  —Individual needs for personal growth and development; and
  —The training needed to match these two.
- Training delivers the means by which people acquire additional attributes, or enhance the ones they already have.
- To make the very best of the people in the organization, it seems obvious that there should be the closest possible match between the job profile and the personal profile.
- There are three key aspects of a cost benefit analysis:
  —All the profits of the organization are produced by the efforts of people.
  —The people are paid, and provided with the resources they need to do their work.
  —The organization invests in training in order to improve the performance of its people.
- The complete performance management system is created in three stages:
  —Structured task analysis to develop job profiles.
  —Personal attribute profiling.
  —Training resource profiling and delivery.

Glossary of terms

This glossary has been prepared as a means of adding an easy reference to some of the terms used in the book. Some of the definitions have been expanded within the book, others have been defined here rather than in the text where they appear.

Application system	This term refers to the computer system that is used by the computer user to perform some desired task. The system used to control the computer is called the 'operating system'.
Artificial intelligence	The process by which a computer can reason and 'learn' from the activities it undertakes.
Aspiration statement	In personal motivation coaching (see Chapter 7) individuals are asked to assess their aspirations, and to write a general summary of them; this is their 'aspiration statement'.
Attribute deviations	When the attributes required by a specific job are compared with the attributes held by a particular person, there is likely to be a difference. This difference is referred to as the 'attribute deviations'.
Attribute profiles	'Attribute profiles' can be created for people, and for jobs. They describe the knowledge, skills, attitudes and behaviour that are needed by people to perform specific jobs, or that are currently held by people.
Barriers	We all have barriers to our personal growth, most of which have been forged in our childhood by continuous conditioning. These are the 'barriers' referred to in the text.
Boundaries	During our development as people we have been conditioned to accept many boundaries, and areas that are 'out of bounds'. To develop a 'no limits' approach we have to expand, or remove the 'boundaries' to our growth.
Breathing space	We never have enough time to stop and think about ourselves, and our lives. We all need a 'breathing space', either by ourselves, or with a counsellor.
Building blocks	To grow and develop as individuals we all need to know and understand our strengths. It is these strengths which form the 'building blocks' to our future.

CCBT — CCBT is an abbreviation for Concurrent Computer Based Training, and is one of the new training tools (see Chapter 16). It is a means whereby a training system can be built to run concurrently with an application system, thus giving the learner, or new user continuous help and support.

Continuous training and support — This phrase is used to refer to any process whereby the learner receives information and support when and where they need it, both during training and on the job. In this book it refers particularly to technology-based training.

Cost benefit model — The relationship of costs to benefits is very important in training. The financial framework by which this relationship is described is the 'cost benefit model'.

Decision trees — A 'decision tree' is a technique for helping to evaluate the probabilities of possible outcomes when making a decision.

Dialogue management — When a computer is interacting with the user it is necessary for every input and response to be carefully logged and controlled by the computer. This process is referred to as 'dialogue management'.

Digital signal — This is a electrical pulse, or sound wave that represents one part of a sound, word, or picture. It might be represented as a magnetized spot on a magnetic disc, or as an equivalent mark on an optical disc.

Dynamic learning — A technique where the learner is exposed to a learning opportunity that is constantly changing (see Chapter 7).

ECBT — ECBT is an abbreviation for Embedded Computer Based Training. This is a form of training that is actually built into the application system (see Chapter 16).

Enquiry learning — When people are placed in the position of learning through questioning, they are partaking in 'enquiry learning', which is a technique for constructing learning opportunities that rely on the learner's inherent curiosity.

Expert systems — Computer systems that enable a user to obtain information in the form of advice, together with the reasoning behind the advice, are called 'expert systems'. They have a knowledge base, an inference engine (a set of rules built by a subject expert), and an interface with the user (see Chapter 16).

Flowcharting — 'Flowcharting' is a technique for analysing, or displaying interrelated activities, events, and segments of a training programme. It is widely used in computer systems analysis, but not so widely used in training.

Functionality — Computer application systems provide the user with a range of things that they can do. It is this range of computer capability that is referred to as 'functionality'.

Human–machine interface — The point at which a human being uses a computer is the 'human–machine interface'. It is not a thing; it is a point in time and space where interaction occurs between the person and the machine. The nature of this interaction is a vital factor in the design of easy-to-use computer systems.

Interactive Help — One of the key elements of ECBT is 'interactive Help'. It is a process where information is built into the application system so that it is available when the user wants it without the need to refer to any external paper-based manuals.

Learning-centred design — Training is the process of helping people to learn. To build training programmes that do this effectively it is desirable to place the learning at the centre of the design. 'Learning-centred design' is the process by which this is done.

Learning-desire — The most effective learning takes place when the learners actually want to learn. This desire to learn is very powerful, so creating 'learning-desire' becomes a key part of 'learning-centred design'.

Learning domain — The subject area in which the learning is to take place is referred to as the 'learning domain'.

Learning interaction — When people learn they interact with the environment in which they are learning. This interaction may be questioning a teacher, experimenting with some object, playing, and so on. Any and all of these interactions are referred to as a 'learning interaction'.

Learning-management — The learning process can take place in a completely unstructured way, and this would be called 'natural learning'. When learning takes place as a result of some training intervention the process is managed, and we call this activity 'learning-management'.

Learning-need statement — A 'learning need statement' is a written description of the learning needs that can be satisfied from taking advantage of a particular 'learning opportunity'.

Learning opportunity — Any training programme provides learners with the opportunity to learn. Instead of referring to such opportunities as training, implying that the learners will 'receive' training, I prefer to use the description of 'learning opportunity'.

Learning path — The 'learning path' is the route that the learner will follow through the 'learning terrain'.

Learning process — When learning takes place a number of things happen. Learners find that they go through at least three stages: appreciating what they want to learn; understanding what they want to learn; and finally being able to perform. The activities that take place during learning are referred to as the 'learning process'.

Learning psychology — The 'learning process' involves the use of our inherent learning skills. The way we use these skills, and our understanding of the mental activities that take place are referred to as 'learning psychology'.

Learning targets
When learners start out on the learning journey they usually have some target in mind. These 'learning targets' form the basis for evaluating the success of the training.

Learning terrain
The particular section of the 'learning domain' which is being dealt with in a particular 'learning opportunity', is referred to as the 'learning terrain'.

Life-cycle investment
When appraising the training investment it is important to take into account the whole of the life cycle of the training programme, and not just the initial establishment costs. The technique for doing this is called 'life-cycle investment'.

Local area networks
Communication systems that allow computers to be linked together within a single location are called 'local area networks' or LANs.

Objectives/impact statement
This term refers to the preparation of a statement for each employee of their personal objectives, and the impact they have on the profits of the organization.

Optical cable
Light can be passed along special cable made of optical fibres. This is called 'optical cable'.

Optical discs
Digital signals can now be recorded on 'optical discs' which are read by laser beams. This allows data and pictures to be stored in large volumes, and read at very high speeds.

Personal affirmations
A 'personal affirmation' is a statement which encourages people to believe in themselves, and to reinforce their self-esteem.

Personal motivation coaching
In Chapter 7 I describe a technique whereby people can develop and grow by removing the barriers and boundaries that constrain them. This technique I have called 'personal motivation coaching'.

Performance index
When measuring performance it is important to have a measure that relates performance to some pre-established target. The 'performance index' is such a measure, e.g. the percentage of correct transactions to total transactions would be a 'performance index'.

Performance standard
'Performance indices' need to have an agreed value attached to them. Such values are 'performance standards'.

Policy and procedure manual
When ECBT is used there is less need for the traditional user guides and methods manuals. There is still a need for reference to information that is not part of the ECBT system, and this is where the 'policy and procedure manual' is used.

Positive learning
This is a technique where the emphasis is placed on doing things in the right way, as against showing people how not to do things. It has been popular for

a long time to teach people by showing them the effects of doing things the wrong way. 'Positive learning' redresses the balance.

Potential profile
In 'personal motivation coaching' people are asked to prepare a statement of their strengths, and their personal potential as they see it. This is their 'potential profile'.

Simulation
An exact replica of the situation learners will meet in the working environment, or as near a facsimile as can be produced.

Software packages
A set of computer programs produced and sold as a complete package for carrying out a specified task, i.e. a word processing package.

Structured task analysis
This is the first part of the learning-centred design methodology, and seeks to break down the job being performed into separate tasks, so that the attributes needed to perform the job can be determined.

Systematized
When a particular activity, or series of activities, is analysed and built into a computer system, it is referred to as having been 'systematized'.

Test, pilot, evaluate
This is the final module of the learning centred design methodology, and deals with the process of making sure that the training programme achieves the desired result.

Training data base
When training is built into the computer it is necessary to build a data base that is specifically for training use. This is called the 'training data base'. The way to construct the 'training data base' is covered in module four of the ECBT methodology.

Training investment appraisal
When a training project is being considered it is important to make sure that the investment is worth while from a financial point of view. This is the purpose of the 'training investment appraisal', which is a financial evaluation technique.

Training module attribute analysis
When building a performance management system it is essential to know which attributes each training programme addresses. As each job is broken down into the attributes needed to perform successfully, it is valuable to be able to relate the training available to the attributes addressed. This is the purpose of 'training module attribute analysis'.

Training programme development
This is the fourth module of the learning centred design methodology, the outcome of which is the complete training programme design report.

Training screen definition
When Help is being written for ECBT it is essential to have a complete understanding of each computer screen used in the system for which training is being developed. The 'training screen definition' is the method used to provide the information needed.

Training competency analysis — In the learning-centred design methodology, when the task analysis has been completed it is important to decide how performance of the task is to be measured. This, the second module of the learning-centred design methodology, provides a step-by-step procedure for measuring performance.

Training window — This term is used to describe the small area of the computer screen where information is provided on top of the application screen. Windows can appear anywhere on the screen, and sometimes it is effective to use more than one window at the same time. It is used in both ECBT and CCBT, and many software packages include the window feature.

Tutorials — 'Tutorials' are used in ECBT and CCBT to give information and explanation, and to offer learners the opportunity to assess their progress. They may include simulations, demonstrations, and exercises.

Usability — This term describes the degree to which a computer system is easy to use.

Validation routines — In computer systems many checks are carried out by the computer to validate the data being input. The sequence of steps followed by the computer system when making these checks is referred to as the 'validation routine'.

Note

If more information is required about:

TOUCH
ECBT
CCBT
ACE
CASE

then please contact the author

Dr Trevor Bentley
The Bungalow
Harewood Road
Collingham
Wetherby
West Yorkshire
LS22 5BZ

Suggested reading

Bach, Richard, *Illusions*, London: Pan Books, 1978.
A small and powerful commentary on the human search for personal power.

Bach, Richard, *Jonathan Livingston Seagull*, London: Pan Books, 1973.
Simply brilliant, both in its clarity and the message of personal self-belief. The power we all have knows no limits.

Carson, Richard D, *Taming Your Gremlin*, New York: Harper & Row, 1983.
This book has been a great help in making me realize that my reaction to people when I am training is often controlled for the worst by my gremlin which I have now put away in chains.

Fulghum, Robert, *All I Really Need to Know I Learned in Kindergarten*, New York: Villard Books, 1986.
A lovely book, full of fascinating insights to the learning process, and a reminder that training is helping people to learn.

Gawain, Shakti, *Creative Visualization*, USA: Whatever Publishing, 1979.
If you think affirmations are ineffective read and practise the ideas in this book and it will change your life as it has mine.

Gawain, Shakti, *Living in the Light*, USA: Whatever Publishing, 1986.
Even better than Shakti's first book.

Gery, Gloria, *Making CBT Happen*, Boston: Weingarten, 1988.
An excellent book by a good friend of mine. It is very clear about the advantages and disadvantages of CBT, and gives a good guide on how to use CBT effectively.

Giles, Lionel, *The Sayings of Lao Tzu*, London: John Murray, 1905.
A small book with a powerful message that underlies most of my thinking, the way I write, and the way I work.

Heider, John, *The Tao of Leadership*, Aldershot: Wildwood House, 1986.
Quite a brilliant book. Essential reading for everyone who aspires to be a trainer or leader. It is based on the sayings of Lao Tzu.

Hoff, Benjamin, *The Tao of Pooh*, London: Methuen, 1982.
Another splendid book about the simple things in life that we so often forget.

Holt, John, *How Children Learn*, London: Penguin Books, 1984.
A standard text for teachers, which should become a standard text for trainers, for the lessons to learn are the same. Adults don't learn differently from children; we have just forgotten how to learn properly.

Jackins, Harvey, *The Nature of the Learning Process*, Washington: Rational Island, 1966.
A few pages of the most powerful words ever written about learning.

Jampolsky, Gerald G, *Teach Only Love*, New York: Bantam Books, 1983.
The ability to treat all people in a caring and loving way is crucial to successful training. This book offers an excellent guide to how to love unconditionally.

Kolb, David A, *Experiential Learning*, New Jersey: Prentice-Hall, 1984.
The message is about experience being the great teacher, but argued with much more conviction and empirical evidence than Mumford's book (see below).

Lake, Tony and Fran Acheson, *Room to Listen Room to Talk*, London: Bedford Square Press, 1988.
An excellent little introduction to counselling.

Mumford, Alan, *Making Experience Pay*, Maidenhead: McGraw-Hill, 1980.
A good reminder that the majority of what we learn is via actually doing and experiencing things.

Paulus, Trina, *Hope for the Flowers*, New York: Paulist Press, 1982.
A lovely reminder that we are all in danger of forgetting the good things in life in our pursuit of success.

Pryor, Karen, *Don't Shoot the Dog*, New York: Bantam Books, 1985.
This is about training animals and the comparison with training humans. More a book about conditioning, but still worth reading.

Rodgers, Carl, *Carl Rodgers on Personal Power*, London: Constable, 1978.
This book is brilliant. If you want to increase your personal power in getting your life right for you this is the starting place.

Rodgers, Carl, *Freedom to Learn for the 80's*, Columbus: Charles E. Merrill, 1983.
This book has been the inspiration to my work over the last few years. I am a disciple of Carl Rodgers. I think this book is fabulous.

Index